HOW TO SET UP & RUN YOUR OWN BUSINESS

The Daily Telegraph
A BUSINESS ENTERPRISE BOOK

HOW TO SET UP & RUN YOUR OWN BUSINESS

Seventh Edition

KOGAN PAGE

Published by Kogan Page Limited, 120 Pentonville Road, London N1 9JN for Telegraph Publications, Peterborough Court, at South Quay, 181 Marsh Wall, London E14 9SR

First published 1983
Reprinted May 1983
Second edition October 1983
Third edition May 1984
Fourth edition April 1985
Fifth edition June 1986
Sixth edition 1987
Seventh edition 1989

British Library Cataloguing in Publication Data
How to set up and run your own business – 7th edition
1. Great Britain. Small firms. Organisation
I. Series
658′.022′0941

ISBN 1–85091–993–3
ISBN 1–85091–994–1 pbk

Fourth, fifth, sixth and seventh editions edited by Redfern Publishing Services.

Typeset at The Spartan Press Ltd, Lymington, Hants
Printed by Biddles Ltd, Guildford

THE CONTRIBUTORS

We would like to express our appreciation of the help given by the following contributors in the preparation of this book.

Hugh Aldous
partner, Robson Rhodes

John Anisworth
secretary, The Institute of Administrative Management

Henry Ballantyne
industrial relations consultant; and member, IPM national employee relations committee

Carol Barrie
partner, Peat, Marwick, Mitchell

Geoffrey Burcher
partner, Collier, Bigwood and Bewlay

John Blundell
director of public affairs, Institute of Humane Studies

Norman Boakes
senior partner, Euro Marketors Partnership; past national chairman, Institute of Marketing

Roy Chapman
managing partner London, Arthur Andersen & Co

Representatives from the Charterhouse Group

Colin Davis
tax partner, Spicer and Pegler

Robert Fleeman
director, Smaller Businesses Advisory Services

Andrew Hamilton
partner, Binder Hamlyn

Charles Hodder
manager, transport administration, Dunlop Ltd, tyre division

Keith Jones
associate, Collier, Bigwood and Bewlay

Jim Kerevan
partner, Peat, Marwick, Mitchell

Michael Killingley
senior manager, Peat, Marwick, Mitchell

Richard Lee
assistant director of training, Arthur Andersen & Co

Bill Packer
national tax technical director, Touche Ross & Co

David Philips
partner in charge of small business monitoring, Robson Rhodes

Michael Reader
senior tax manager, Peat, Marwick, Mitchell

Frank Rounthwaite
partner-in-charge Birmingham, Robson Rhodes

Tony Timberlake
managing partner Birmingham, Arthur Andersen & Co

Michael Tomlinson
partner, Thornton Baker

Frank Walker
head of data processing (consultant), Thornton Baker

Rodney Westhead
partner, Thornton Baker

Ken White
(K & J Consultants), The Institute of Administrative Management

David Wise
director, Binder Hamlyn Fry

H H Yates
chairman of council, The Institute of Export

David Young
trade development manager, National Westminster Bank, international division

Contents

CAR CONTRACT HIRE THAT PUTS SMALL BUSINESSES IN THE DRIVING SEAT

Venture Contract is low cost flexible contract hire. Not only does it remove much of the hassle involved in ownership or leasing but it does so for around 75% of normal contract hire rates! And there are even short term options from as little as 3 months.

For the full story on Venture Contract, send for our information pack or call Allison Stephens on 01-993 7611 or your nearest regional office.

VENTURE CONTRACT

CAR CONTRACT HIRE THAT COSTS LESS

Venture Hire Limited, Wincanton House, 333 Western Avenue, London W3 ORS.
Telephone 01-993 7611. Fax 01-993 0990.
Tel: Manchester 061 872 8911. Tel: Birmingham 021 702 2940

Foreword

I am delighted to introduce the seventh edition of *How to Set Up and Run Your Own Business*. If you are starting your own business this book will be a valuable asset.

All those who wish to start their own business should take up-to-date professional advice and I commend this book to them as an excellent starting point.

There are a variety of agencies which can offer further help and guidance. In particular, I recommend the Government's Small Firms Service (SFS) which can be contacted by dialling 100 and asking for Freefone Enterprise. The SFS, besides providing up-to-the-minute business information, can also offer professional business counselling. In addition, it can direct you to other sources of help including Enterprise Agencies, the Department of Trade and Industry's 'Enterprise Initiative', the British Overseas Trade Board and the new Training and Enterprise Councils to be set up over the next few years.

I congratulate the Daily Telegraph on this latest edition of its comprehensive guide. I wish all its readers success and I am sure this book will help them achieve it.

THE RT HON JOHN COPE MP
Minister for Small Firms
Department of Employment

Introduction

This book is a very basic introduction to the world of the self-employed and the small businessman. It has been written on the assumption that you have spent your working life to date as an employee, and that your knowledge of VAT, National Insurance and such matters is limited.

There are over three million people in business on their own today. Two and a quarter million are self-employed, and the remainder are directors of their own limited companies. Large numbers of people every month are setting up in business. Some 96 per cent of all firms are small businesses, accounting for 20 per cent of our gross national product. With big business laying people off, and cuts in local and central government, what is left for you to do? Either work for a small business or start up on your own.

So what do these small business people do? By far the most popular area is the retail sector, followed by the building industry. Wherever there is a gap in the market, you are likely to find self-employed people trying to satisfy the demand for goods and services. From the shopkeeper, the builder and the farmer to the self-employed tobacco-taster and the self-employed golf course designer – you name it, the self-employed are doing it.

Have you a viable proposition?

Two essential elements in a viable business proposition are the product (or service) and the people involved. Until the marketability of the product has been established, there is little point in proceeding further, but given a commercial product and a good management team, it will then be necessary to look carefully at the premises, equipment and financial resources necessary to start the business.

It is tempting to think that a novel idea has better prospects than a proven product; in practice it is not as simple as that.

If you plan to sell your product or service to an established market, are you sure that your sales projections are realistic for a business starting from scratch? You need to consider the size of the total market, whether it is expanding or contracting, the number of competitors active in it already and how the market is divided among them. Ask yourself what proportion of the market the new enterprise aims to capture in the first year, the second year and so on, and why people should buy from you instead of from someone else. How sensitive are your projections to the impact of a fairly small variation in market share achievements?

Finally, in reviewing your product, make sure that you have the legal right to produce and sell it. Legal advice may be necessary in order to safeguard the future of your project.

What kind of business?

Let us begin by looking at the initial stages of starting a business. If you are setting up as a sole trader, say a freelance consultant, with a turnover below the VAT threshold, no premises and no staff, and you are trading under your own name, then virtually all you have to do is tell the Inland Revenue and the Department of Social Security of your change in status, and then begin to trade. However, once you reach the VAT threshold, use separate business premises, take on staff and trade perhaps as a limited company, the picture is very different.

The sole trader

The first question you need to ask yourself is, what

form will my business take? The simplest way of going into business is to trade on your own and under your own name. The main point to bear in mind is that you are personally liable for all debts since you have no limited liability.

However, you may feel that your name is not the most striking, or the most easily remembered, so you may decide to trade under a name other than your own. In this case as the name is not your own and therefore ownership of the business is not immediately apparent, it is necessary to show in three places your name and an address within Great Britain at which the service of documents will be effective. This must appear on all letters, orders, invoices, receipts and written demands for payments, and must be prominently displayed at all places in which the business is conducted, and to which customers and suppliers have access. You have what is known as a general statutory duty to divulge ownership of the business and an effective address within Great Britain at which a document may be served upon you. This you may have to do on demand, in writing. Even though you are trading under a name which is not your own, you are still personally liable for all debts.

Going into partnership

The same statutory rules apply to a partnership as to the sole trader, the main difference being that you are working with someone else and not by yourself. It is also worth remembering that should your partner amass debts, unknown to you, then in all likelihood you will be responsible for those debts if your partner disappears.

A partnership agreement will need to be drawn up by a solicitor in order to prevent difficulties arising from any future break-up of the partnership. This agreement needs to cover the basis on which the partners intend to work together, and should among other stipulations include:

— The procedures to be followed should one of the

partners die or leave the business for any other reason;
— Definition of the partners' remuneration;
— Whether decisions are made jointly or separately.

If you are going into a partnership or starting up as a sole trader, remember that the statutory benefits to the self-employed, sickness benefit, for example, are considerably less than those for the employed. Permanent Health Insurance (PHI) policies, pensions, etc. all need to be considered. Ask your insurance broker to submit a number of quotes from different insurance companies.

The limited company

The main difference between trading as a company and trading as a partnership is the limited liability factor. The directors of a company are not personally liable for debts incurred by the company except for non-payment of NI contributions. Everyone's circumstances are different and there are different schools of thought; if you are thinking of going into business and of forming a limited company, get advice from an accountant or solicitor first. Do not rush into it without thought and good reasons.

There are four main matters to be dealt with in forming a company (in some instances your solicitor will be able to help):

— Choosing a name;
— Defining the business purpose of the company (its 'objects');
— Settling its contribution and procedural rules (the company's 'Memorandum and Articles of Association');
— Filing particulars with the Registrar of Companies, Companies Registration Office, Crown Way, Maindy, Cardiff CF4 3UZ; you can ask your solicitor to deal with this for you. (Details required are the company's registered office, particulars of shareholders, directors and company secretary.)

The co-operative

The concept of the co-operative is undergoing a revival, with a recent dramatic upsurge in the number formed. You now find co-operatives trading in many types of industry, from manufacturing to retail. In September 1978, Parliament established the Co-operative Development Agency (01–839 2988) on a national scale (see Appendix IV). It offers advice on how to find your local co-operative development agency, how to set up and run your own co-operative, appraisal of specific projects including assessment of the product, its market and advice on legal and taxation problems, education and training, sources of finance, etc.

A workers' co-operative is one which is owned and democratically run by its members, who are mainly employees. All members have equal voting rights although not all decisions are taken at a mass meeting with a show of hands. Responsibility for the various business disciplines is distributed to each of the members, giving them sole control in their particular sections.

Co-operatives come in many different forms, from the workers' co-operative through to the community co-operative. Whatever form it takes, the basis of a co-operative is that the business is entirely owned and ultimately controlled by the workforce.

'That is all very well, but why form a co-operative?' The prime consideration in starting any form of business is whether it is going to be a viable concern. The advantage of the co-operative is that responsibility for the business is shared, while at the same time each individual member is putting up some form of collateral (possibly equal amounts), so that resources are pooled and abilities used to the full.

If your co-operative has less than 20 members it can begin life without having to be a registered, incorporated organisation. But as soon as it functions with a view to making a profit, it becomes a partnership and therefore is not encompassed by the limited liability protection of a limited company. The co-operative can be incorporated into a limited company, or it can be registered under the Industrial and Provident Societies Acts, in which case its annual returns will be sent to the Registrar. In most cases the co-operative would be liable to corporation tax.

When setting up a co-operative, the Memorandum and Articles of Association are vital, and detailed discussion with your fellow-workers and your solicitor is advisable. However, it would be best to talk first to the Co-operative Development Association, who supply full details not only of areas of assistance but also about its formation.

Selling to your market

The golden rule when you are going into business is to be very, very careful. You may have come to grips with VAT and approaching financiers, but have you really thought objectively about your product or service? Do it now before it is too late.

Marketing encompasses a wide selection of disciplines from market research to public relations, and its overall policy should be followed through in each of the separate sections, including sales (see Chapter 4).

Market research

Before you go any further, check the area that you are planning to go into. Check the demand for your product or service, and if there is no direct competition, ask yourself, 'Why not?' Does a suitable market-place exist? If you know your industry, take a sample of companies, speak to their buyers and see if they would be interested in purchasing your product; then ask yourself whether these expressions of interest could materialise into actual sales. Be cautious and honest with yourself in answering. Write down any query you may have and make sure that it can be answered. Above all, make sure that there is actually a demand in the market-place for your products.

Publicity

Many people starting off in business think that they are going to be spending a lot of money on advertising, but this is not always so. Take the typical example of one manufacturer who spent £5,000 on advertising in the trade press in the spring. It brought him only about 100 sales leads, and very few of those were converted into actual sales. In the autumn his business had a new product to offer and he launched it with a press release to the same trade papers. The press release was well received, and as a result it was written up. This article led to several hundred sales leads, of which a far higher percentage has now been converted into sales. So do not think that because you are going into business, you simply have to pick the right media to advertise in: there are various ways and means of advertising within each medium, some more cost-effective than others, and it is worth giving some thought to the matter.

Consider another example of a man who imported a book on Japanese flower-arranging. He did a bit of research about where his market lay, and he found that there was in fact a Society of Japanese Flower-Arrangers who had a small magazine which was circulated to 1,500 people each month. To advertise in this magazine cost £6 a page, and for this he was reaching all his potential customers.

Then there was the man who made flying helmets for people who drove open sports cars. Instead of advertising in a national or regional paper, which can be very expensive, he advertised solely in magazines produced by the MG, Jaguar and Morgan sports car clubs. These magazines go to precisely the people to whom he wants to sell his products: the people who drive open sports cars. The message is: think very carefully about the way in which you are going to promote your business. Do not be lured by the glamour of the advertising world if it is not right for you.

Franchising

Franchising is becoming more and more popular today, and among the many well-known names are Home Tune, ServiceMaster, Kentucky Fried Chicken and Wimpy. It begins when somebody has a bright idea that cannot be promoted by a big business with one or two big outlets because it needs a number of small outlets all over the country. Instead of setting up a lot of little shops or outlets with managers, the franchise operator licenses you for a particular area and then gives you support, technical advice and equipment and in return you pay him a set amount of money.

What are the advantages of franchising? Risk can never be eliminated but franchising does tend to minimise it if you are going in with a tried and tested product. The franchise operator will probably have a lot more business experience than you – or one hopes he has – and he will not allow you to set up in business with his product in a new area unless he is pretty certain that you are going to succeed. The last thing he wants is lots of people trying his franchise operations and failing. There is the added advantage that you have independence with backing. Although you are self-employed and your own boss, you have the support of a larger organisation which gives you continuing assistance and guidance. For instance, national advertising, technical back-up and training is available from a number of franchise operators. Often too, you will be able to work for a period of weeks or months with an existing franchise operator to learn the ropes before you set up on your own.

Management buy-outs

A management buy-out offers an alternative to the complete closure of a business concern and the consequent redundancy of the workforce. The idea is, as the term suggests, for the owners to withdraw from the business completely, leaving it ready for the purchase and reconstruction with another or reorganised management team, into a viable concern.

Like any other business, a 'management buy-out' will succeed if there is a credible, strong management team coupled with a viable business proposition and sufficient funds. Each buy-out situation is unique and professional advice is essential.

Tax matters

National Insurance

As an employed person you will have been paying Class 1 National Insurance contributions, calculated as a percentage of your income, with your employer paying as well on your behalf. For this you will have been entitled to the full range of DSS benefits. However, as a self-employed person you are on your own, possibly having to pay your contributions in two ways (see Chapter 7). If you are trading as a partnership or are not receiving a salary then your payment structure will alter and you will not be entitled to the full range of benefits. Many self-employed people have their own private health cover and pensions to make up for this.

If you have set up a limited company, you are in effect your own employer, so you pay NI both as an employer and as an employee. The limited liability cover does not protect you against non-payment of contributions. Company directors are personally liable for non-payment of NI contributions.

Paying tax

In a nutshell, you pay tax in any one year on the profits from the previous year (see Chapter 7). There are many complicated rules governing both the opening and the closing years of your business accounts, as well as whether or not you are trading as a company or as a sole trader/partnership. There are considerable advantages in choosing your accounting date and form of business carefully, so before you do anything, please obtain professional advice.

Much is made of the tax advantages of being self-employed. As an employee everything has been provided for you by your company: from a desk and paperclips, to a car, perhaps, and pencils. Now you will have to provide all that for yourself. All that Schedule D allows you to do is offset such costs before calculating the income on which you are to be taxed. If you plan to run a car half for business and half for pleasure then 50 per cent of the cost for business will be allowable. If you purchase a car with a loan, and use this car on company business, then you are allowed tax relief on the loan interest.

Value added tax

Now perhaps one of the most dreaded subjects of all – VAT. If you are going to be running a pub or a shop or manufacturing business, then you will almost certainly be forced into VAT, since your turnover will probably be over £23,600 per annum – the 1989/90 VAT limit above which you have to register for and pay VAT, (or exceed £8,000, the quarterly maximum allocation on two or more occasions). If you are a one-man-band your turnover may not be so high, in which case you have a choice as to whether or not you choose to register. But if inadvertently you go over the VAT registration levels and have not registered and do not charge VAT, then you will face severe penalties.

The Chancellor of the Exchequer in his 1987 Budget announced further changes to the consultative paper. These changes have now been ratified under article 27 of the EEC 6th VAT Directive, and are noted accordingly in Chapters 6 and 7.

How does VAT work? It is what is called a payment and reclaim system. At the end of each quarter you add up how much VAT you have collected from your customers. Take the case of a trader who has collected £700 but during the same quarter has himself been charged £200 in VAT, having bought a desk, some petrol, office equipment and various other supplies. Within a month of the end of the quarter, the trader has to hand over to the Customs and Excise a completed VAT quarterly return along with the difference between the £700 and the £200, namely £500. Most goods and services are rated at 15 per cent. However, there are two main exceptions. The zero-rated trader (some businesses such as farms, chemists and publishers are zero-rated), instead of putting VAT at 15 per cent on the end of the bill, can put VAT at zero. At the end of the quarter the zero-rated trader has collected from his customers zero pounds but in the same quarter he has probably (as in our previous example) been charged VAT on petrol and other supplies and he has, say, paid out £200 in VAT. He still does the same sum, but this time £200 will be repaid to him by the Customs and Excise. Because that money is paid back, the zero-rated trader is often referred to as the 'repayment trader'.

The other main exception is the exempt trader. The government has decided that certain trades and professions are exempt from VAT – for example, nursing homes and insurance brokers. These people are not allowed into the VAT club, regardless of their turnover. They are just like the ordinary man in the street, but they have to pay VAT on everything they buy and they cannot reclaim it, nor can they put VAT on their bills.

Learning about the law

Employment law

As your business expands you will find the need for assistance, so you employ a person to help you in the office and in so doing you are now taking on a member of staff. Within 13 weeks of taking on this person, you have to supply him or her with a written Contract of Employment. Briefly, this has to cover the names of the parties involved, the date that employment began, the rate of pay and the method of calculating pay; the terms and conditions need to include normal working hours, holiday entitlement, sickness entitlement, pension entitlement, job title, notice provisions, the company's disciplinary rules and the name of the person to go to if there is any grievance or any appeal about disciplinary decisions.

Small businesses are now much more favourably treated under the employment law than in previous years. It is only when an employee has worked for his employer for two years that legal employee rights, such as unfair dismissal and redundancy, apply. Should you employ fewer than five people then you are not legally required to grant maternity rights and maternity pay. (If an employee is self-employed, however, and has paid sufficient contributions, then the Maternity Allowance can be claimed.)

The Department of Employment issues a series of about 20 leaflets covering every possible aspect of employment law, from redundancy and unfair dismissal to contracts and maternity leave.

There is also the Health and Safety at Work Act to consider. Breach of this law is a serious offence which can lead to prosecution and, if successful in a high court, unlimited fines. The purpose of the Act is to provide, promote, and encourage high standards of health and safety at the place of work.

Planning law and premises

Planning law is another area on which you will need to be informed. If you work at home but are often out visiting clients, and you do not have many business visitors and your type of work does not produce any noises or smells, then you will probably be all right. But do check the freehold and leasehold deeds on your house because you might find that there is a very strict clause which completely prohibits any form of business activity from your home; for most people, however, this will not be the case. It will also be necessary to check with your local planning department.

Once you start creating a noise or smell then it is a different matter. It is acceptable, for example, to mend your car in your garage as a hobby, but once you turn your hobby into a business and there are three or four cars parked in your drive and in the road outside your house then that is quite a different matter. Also, if your new business is amazingly successful and the quiet of your suburban cul-de-sac is ruined as 30 or 50 people a day start to beat a path to your door to demand your services or your product, then again you will run into planning problems.

On the legal side, there is also a mass of legislation governing business signs. You cannot go about slapping up signs saying that you are now in business and offering particular services – not even one sign giving your company name.

One thing is certain, you will need to locate your business somewhere and if it is not possible to operate from home then you will have to find a suitable place. How much can you afford to pay and is that a realistic amount for your area? Does your business necessitate you being in the High Street or will a less expensive location be satisfactory? What sorts of property are available in your area? If you are close to a motorway, how important is its location for you? Once you have answered these questions, the next step is to visit local firms of surveyors or estate agents to obtain information from them (see Chapter 3). As with most things, be cautious and seek professional advice.

Four case histories

Let us look now very briefly at how four different people started up in business, and how those critical first twelve months went.

1. John Phillips is a graphic designer in Peacehaven in Sussex. He set up a year ago and after a few months his wife gave up her job and joined him, then a few months ago he took on his first employee. When he set up he thought he would be spending 95 per cent of his time on the drawing board and only 5 per cent of the time out getting work and dealing with customers. In fact he has found that he spends only about 50 per cent of his time at the drawing board, with the other 50 per cent spent looking for work, delivering it, checking it over with clients, and dealing with clients on the telephone. His wife now runs the administrative side of the business, does the invoicing, billing, tax, National Insurance and so on, and he has had to employ a full-time graphic artist who spends all his time at the drawing board.

2. Sandra Gardiner is from Ripon in North Yorkshire. She thought she spotted a gap in the market a year ago, noting that there were a lot of self-employed businessmen in the area, many of whom needed perhaps a few hours of secretarial help a week. However, they could not afford and did not need a full-time secretary. She looked around and found that there was no secretarial agency offering this sort of service. So in the middle of last year she set up a business, offering secretarial services to small businessmen. She started off by making herself known through the local National Federation of Self-Employed branch, the local National Farmers' Union branch, the Chamber of Commerce and other similar organisations, explaining that her services were available and that they were specially geared to the local small businessman. The work has come in and she has not needed to advertise or do anything more. Sandra considers that a good job delivered on time and well done means that she gets more work by recommendation.

3. Richard Reynolds from Lewisham, in South London, went into the army when he was 15 and eight years later came out as a fully trained mechanic. He had always wanted his own small garage but he did not rush into it. First, he spent a year working for another small garage. Although he already knew how to repair, store and maintain cars, he did not know anything about running a small garage. He also spent that year considering how he would make his service different from that of all other small garages. He decided to concentrate on repairing and restoring old sports cars, since he thought that in London and the South East there was a market for such a service. He found that setting up always costs more than you think. He also considers that it is important to keep on top of the book

work. He closes his garage at noon on Saturday and spends the whole of the afternoon on his books and does not leave the garage at the weekend until his books are completed. His tip is, don't go planning your holidays just because you had a good week, because next week the turnover will probably be poor.

4. Alex James, again from North Yorkshire, was in middle management in Harrogate, but he attended a 'Be Your Own Boss' seminar and decided to become self-employed. His business is the collection and same-day delivery of small parcels – documents and valuable items – throughout North Yorkshire. After nearly a year he has two vehicles. He advises new entrepreneurs not to rely on promises of work in the early stages. In the first three months he went round all the companies he knew in the area and many of them said, 'Oh yes, Alex, you set up and we are sure that we will be able to find you lots of work.' So he started up, and went back, but all those promises disappeared. People began to say: 'Come back in a fortnight; we haven't got anything this week, but maybe next week.' And for the first three months he spent 95 per cent of his time just knocking on doors to get the work. He had not envisaged that happening; it was not in his cash-flow forecast. At the end of those three months it was touch and go as to whether he would survive. Fortunately, the work started coming in and all his personal calls began to pay off. Now it is the other way round. He spends 95 per cent of his time on the road and only 5 per cent looking for business. Just the occasional leaflet drop around the area is now enough to ensure continued business.

What makes an entrepreneur?

So what sort of qualities do self-employed people need? They have to be healthy, persevering, enterprising, hard-working, unflappable, motivated, confident and independent. If you are going to be self-employed you have to be the sort of person who can cope with a bank manager ringing up in the morning telling you that you have gone over your overdraft limit again. You have to be able to handle irate customers and cope with the VAT or Planning Officer coming in and bothering you at the same time, and be able to get on and do your business as well. If you feel that you will not be able to cope with such stress, then self-employment is not for you.

The first quality noted in the list above was health. As was mentioned earlier, the DSS and National Insurance are none too generous as far as self-employed people go, and so good health is essential. Government statistics show that for every ten days the typical employed person is ill, a self-employed person is ill for only three days. If you are self-employed, you will probably work much longer hours in much tougher circumstances. If you are the sort of person who is not very healthy, with a long record of sickness, then perhaps opening a shop every morning at 8 am and staying open until 6 pm is not for you.

Being self-employed is a risky business and nine out of ten people who set up in business this week will not be running that same business in five years' time. That does not mean that 90 per cent will have gone bankrupt. There are hundreds of reasons – from death to emigration – to explain why a business will not be running in five years' time. There might be the odd business which is obviously going to run into deficit and so is closed down before its owner goes bankrupt. But people do end up losing the roof over their heads, with their houses being put up for sale to pay off their debts, so do think very carefully before risking everything in business. If you are still determined, despite all the warnings and potential hazards, then you are advised to do all your homework first so that you go into business with your eyes wide open.

Conclusion

This book's aim is to alert you to the obvious pitfalls and to encourage you to make a success of your plans. It is based on years of experience. By the time you reach the last chapter you should have a clearer idea of your capabilities and the possibilities for your enterprise. Then you can go on to the Appendix which is packed with useful names, addresses, and further publications to read. There is also some space for you at the end to start up your own essential reference list: your personal directory of names and contacts. A series of checklists is included as a reminder of some of the questions which need to be answered. In Appendix II we have noted some of the financial options open to you. The text has been specially written to emphasise the practical points and relevant actions.

The importance of certain aspects of business are worth special care and attention. Forecasts and budgets are very important and are required (1) to anticipate the likely costs and whether a project is feasible or not and (2) to ensure that costs are kept within the agreed budget. When preparing them, do ensure that you cover all possible expenditure and when estimating your sales forecasts do not be over-generous.

We will cover the different administrative systems in Chapter 6, but a brief word may be useful here on the many types of office equipment. There is a vast range of office equipment; do ensure before you purchase any equipment that you are not being carried away by the salesman's chatter and that you need – and can afford – the photocopier, computer, office furnishings, etc. offered for sale. Remember that it is a highly competitive market and should you want to purchase office equipment, then obtain a number of quotes beforehand.

Throughout the book we emphasise the necessity for professional advice from whatever source, and the government-run Small Firms Service, being readily accessible, is a most useful vehicle, along with many trade associations. A small businessman must be well-informed so it is vitally important that he knows who to turn to for the right sort of advice and assistance. If you are starting a hi-tech company, a chat to your local High Street bank is advisable as most banks now run a service geared not only to small businessmen but to those setting up a hi-tech company. Many people setting out do not know how to compile budgets or estimate their capital requirements – if this is true in your case, then go and talk to your accountant. If you want advice about setting up a company and compiling any documentation necessary to trade, go and see your solicitor. When you buy a second-hand car you pay for the advice of a motoring organisation, so why not do the same when investing in your future prosperity? One businessman, having supposedly considered his plan, set up his business for supplying summer garden plants in November, and for the first four months wondered why business was slow. He had not thought carefully enough; if he had asked questions in the first place he would not have found himself in difficulties. The analysis of whether there is a market for your product and putting your thoughts on this down on paper, is very important. You must be clear in your own mind that your business has a chance to succeed, otherwise how can you co-ordinate the information and then sell your idea to your bank?

Over recent years the importance of small businesses, in relation to the growth of the economy, has been recognised. In order to relieve the small businessman's burden, the government reviewed ways in which the amount of 'red tape', which so often hampers a business, could be reduced.

A final note: every effort has been made to ensure that all the information given here is as up to date as possible. But the world of small business is fast changing, so make sure that you have the latest Inland Revenue, HM Customs and Excise and DSS leaflets to hand, and keep in touch with your local small business information services. And if there is any information you would like to see included in the next edition of this book, please write to the publishers.

1 What types of capital are there?

This chapter is not only about types of capital, but also about some of the principal factors you need to take into consideration in deciding how to finance your business. The following chapter on 'Presenting your case' will guide you through some tried and tested routes.

In financing a small business or raising capital for a new one, you will encounter very differing viewpoints. In the present economic climate the ambitious entrepreneur needs the courage of his convictions, and one of his convictions may well be the infallibility of his idea or project. In other words: 'The banks and other lending establishments should put their money where *my* idea is!' Needless to say this is not often the case.

Those who are in the business of lending money will shake their heads, knowing that in practice the failure rate is high and that most entrepreneurs underestimate the amount of money they will need in order to develop their business – and to learn by their mistakes as they do so. The banks will ask: how much money of your own, or of someone else's, do you have? Who bears the initial risk? Are you going to put your money alongside our money? And if your business goes wrong, how far will you be committed personally?

It is worth understanding these two points of view before studying the capital structure of new businesses and the types of capital and their sources. This is because central to the growth of any business will be the support of a lending banker. The lending banker has a relatively uncomplicated ambition. He looks to gain no more than getting his money back at the end of the period of the loan, and receiving the current market rate of interest on it in the meantime. This does not mean that he will insist on lending risk-free. He will share some risk, but will seek to ensure that the risks of a business are fairly shared between its proprietors and its financial backers.

In a book like this it is not possible to cover in one chapter all types of capital for all types of business. It would take a whole book just to cover sole traders, partnerships and limited companies, and then consider capital for new businesses, development capital for growing existing businesses, and public capital for successful businesses. The assumptions in this chapter are that new businesses need venture capital including equity, existing businesses are profitable enough to need development capital from the banks and that both these businesses are, by and large, limited companies. In fact, in their very early stages, many businesses are unincorporated – often very sensibly so – and they are almost wholly financed on overdrafts supported by personal guarantees and an injection of equity capital by the proprietor(s). This chapter will tend therefore to be about ideals.

Getting the right capital

The most crucial consideration for financing a new business is getting the capital structure right at the beginning. There will doubtless be plenty of other crises as a business develops, without starting out with the kind of finance that cannot sustain the inevitable financial setbacks. Chapter 2 is all about assessing and presenting the case to the banks and explains the projections which you should undertake. Those projections should enable good bankers and good venture capitalists to assess possible ways in which the business may progress, and to judge whether the initial capital is sufficient.

One of the venture capital companies has done some research on the problems of new businesses. Apart from highlighting hopeless management, this research suggests that new manufacturing companies, growing steadily, need cash resources of maybe 25 per cent to 30 per cent of the value of their growing sales in order to finance stocks, debtors (less creditors) and other working capital requirements. If you add to that the capital equipment needed, the initial losses from funding overheads and the product development costs, you will get a severe cash requirement over maybe two or three years. If sufficient capital can be raised in one form or another for the assets of the business, even allowing for initial losses, to be twice the amount which the new business borrows, then that will be more than enough to make sure that further temporary facilities can be arranged to cover any hiccups and delays in cash receipts. The business will then be financially stable.

The problem which faces many small businesses at the outset is under-capitalisation; many lose the confidence of their bankers at their first crisis. It is not the lending banker's job to gamble money on a business where he only gets a market rate of interest on the uncertain outcome of a new venture. Those small businesses are the first ones to fail.

Proprietor's capital

Any business should make sure that it starts life with an adequate base of risk capital. A significant part of that will be the proprietor's capital. Backers, whatever form they take, are more inclined to lend money when they know that the proprietor is doing the same.

There are three sources, at least, for that: the management – you, the one who wants to start or develop his own business; other individuals (friends and associates) subscribing as partners or shareholders; and, for some companies at least, venture capital companies. There are also some sources of quasi-capital: money which is totally at risk and which will only be paid off if the venture is successful (some government project finance is like that).

The individual can borrow his capital, and will

usually get tax relief on the interest. Consequently, if they really believe in their venture, it must be rare for the managing individuals to be unable to raise even a modicum of capital as equity share capital. For others their investments, in companies at least, can provide them with tax relief under the Business Expansion Scheme (BES). This means that there is an extra incentive to subscribe for capital in a new business. That relief has spawned some 30 funds which will pool the subscriptions of individuals and invest the money in new ventures for them.

Then there are the venture capital companies. Each major clearing bank has connections with some of these companies, if it is not connected with one entirely of its own. This form of capital embraces a wide range of potential investments which are not just for high technology companies. The Venture Capital Report (see Appendix IV) publish a guide to venture capital in the United Kingdom. In addition, VCR publish a monthly report which details relative information on small businesses (between five and fifteen per report) who are seeking venture capital. However, it is worth remembering that venture capital is only for businesses who have been incorporated into limited companies.

What venture capital companies will consider doing is financing your business partly with share capital of various types, and partly with loans. If they do a good job they will offset sufficient of the risk which they bear by taking on completely new ventures with the prospect of gain on the few businesses which are successful. This will enable them to offer a high proportion of loan money, and this loan money should be for a sufficiently long term so that the business not only has some financial security for its early years but is still free to finance temporary needs by overdrafts. Sometimes entrepreneurs look on these packages of finance as requiring them to 'give away' some of their equity. That seems an unreasonable view since the investment is not just lending, it is sharing considerable risk.

If you structure the finance of a business properly it will have a greater chance of enabling you to share in most of the prosperity brought by success rather than being left – along with the creditors – with 100 per cent of failure.

A venture capital company will probably draw up an agreement which will further ensure that the business is managed in its interests and that it shares in any profits.

Different kinds of shares

There are various types of shares which might reflect the equity investment in the business.

Ordinary shares

First, the simple ones. This is typical for each share: one equal amount subscribed, one vote, one equal right to any declared dividend. There are all sorts of variations on such ordinary shares. The management's ordinary shares might be deferred as to dividend rights until a certain participation in profit has gone to the other shares. All those other shares, owned by the venture capitalists, might have a right to a special dividend if profits exceed a certain level. As the company's worth increases, so does the value of each share held. It is worth noting, however, that should the business fail, borrowed money has priority for repayment, but only *after* the Revenue and HM Customs and Excise have taken what is owed to them. In businesses where there are sole traders or partnerships, the equity represents any capital introduced plus profits still held in the business.

These are all 'sweeteners' to persuade the investor to provide finance with less of a stake in the equity than if his equity stake had only the same rights as everyone else's. Although this seems quite a good idea, to avoid the feeling of 'giving away' too much of the equity, be careful: if the business is a success it is going to be quite expensive to buy back these shares from the investor who has special profit sharing-rights – even though he did enable the business to get started in the first place.

Shares can be issued under the Business Expansion Scheme to friends and other investors at a premium, whereby more is raised for each of those shares than for the management's own shares. This can prove an attractive way of raising additional share capital for small businesses and can be a tax-efficient way for the investors.

In the 1988 Budget, the Chancellor announced a relief on investments in BES-approved funds by giving investors a relief at the date the investment was made (conditional, however, on at least 90 per cent of the amount being invested in the shares within six months of the closing date each 5 April).

Preference shares

Preference shares are interesting; there are redeemable ones and non-redeemable ones, although the latter are less common. They can strengthen the balance sheet just as well as ordinary shares, but they have a distinct advantage in that they can have reduced voting rights and the proprietors remain in control. Preference shares may have a fixed cumulative dividend to be paid before ordinary shareholders receive their dividends, hence the term 'preference'. They may also have some participation rights in profits above a certain amount. However, it may be that dividends can only be paid if the company is in cumulative profit since starting up. Preference shares can be, and usually are, unsecured, so that the bankers are free to lend against the security of the assets of the business. Unless your business is already prospering, redemption dates on preference shares will probably be left open until the investors are sure that they will get a return.

Where to look for loans

Long-term loans

Generally speaking, long-term loans (ten years or more), i.e. equity capital, are not provided by the clearing banks but are available from other institutions or some subsidiaries of the clearing banks. Banking prudence, and the principle of matching their sources of funds with their assets, mean that clearing banks very rarely lend longer than ten years, unless under a special contract – five to seven years is more usual.

Long-term loans are more likely to be provided by insurance companies, pension funds, Investors in Industry (3i), the Agricultural Mortgage Corporation and the institutions which provide industrial property mortgages, many of whom are also connected with insurance companies. These lenders are looking for a high running yield (high return) on the funds, either because they need that income to meet payments – as the pension funds do – or because that matches the type of finance which they have raised. They require a debenture to secure their loans. If you have a proven track record in running your business it might be possible to negotiate with the lending institution on the matter of how that debenture ranks against the bank, that is, who gets paid first if your enterprise fails. An understanding institution that is prepared to consider a package of loan and equity capital in which the loan is subordinate to an element of bank lending can be a marvellous support to a growing business, but do not expect such support if you have not yet proved yourself.

Contractual term loans are formalised by a specific agreement to cover a specific purpose, period and repayment programme – which might match a cash flow of a project.

Medium-term loans

Medium-term loans are much more home ground for the banks. Every bank has some form of development loan scheme providing five- or seven-year money. Most have some sort of start-up loan scheme by which they will lend money to new businesses, and hope to recover their money and make some sort of extra gain from those which are successful. Most banks also have specific asset loan schemes for specific purchases.

The cost of schemes, if they involve equity options or royalties, may be difficult to quantify, although in general the banks will be looking to charge the equivalent of between 3 and 5 per cent above base rates on the money lent.

The cost of more conventional medium-term finance may be slightly less, and the banks will generally look for security in the form of a fixed or floating charge over the company's assets. Interest margins for larger medium-term loans tend to be between 2 and 4 per cent over base rate. A commitment fee is usually charged and the borrower is required to pay any costs.

The Export Credits Guarantee Department (ECGD) will probably be of invaluable help to any small company seeking to finance its export contracts, because it will open the way to foreign currency lending from the clearing banks.

Instalment credit (hire purchase, in colloquial terms) and leasing have a major application in financing the fixed assets of businesses. Leasing will be the more effective method if taxable profits are not yet anticipated. Instalment credit has now been extended to cover stocking finance for certain industries where the stock items are identifiable.

Factoring provides sales accounting and debt collection services, and some protection against bad debts. Usually some 80 per cent of the debts due to the business is receivable immediately and the balance, less charges, is paid when the debt is recovered. There is a range of other discounting services which tend to be a little expensivc but can relieve the business of time and trouble.

If you are embarking on an export programme, then letters of credit, or bills (see Chapter 10), can be accepted on the London markets and your bank will be able to do this for you.

Revolving credits are rather like household budget accounts, but for companies.

On the face of it the cheapest form of borrowing is often by the simple overdraft. 'Blue chip' companies have frequently enjoyed overdrafts at a margin of 1 per cent above the bank's base rate. Smaller companies usually bear a margin of 2 to 3 per cent, with new companies being charged up to 4 per cent. The rule to remember here is not blindly to accept 4 per cent if another bank will offer you 3.5 per cent – change your bank if necessary. Remember, competition between banks also works to your advantage. On the other hand, your bank manager may offer you a loan at a fixed rate of interest. If interest rates then rise above the rate charged, you are fortunate. However, the reverse can happen. Think very carefully before accepting, should this option be offered.

Many bank managers will have nursed along a new small business on nothing more than an overdraft facility supported by personal guarantees. As a minimum consideration, the overdraft facility should be protected by making sure that 'hard core' overdraft borrowing – that is, the lowest level of borrowing beneath which the overdraft does not go at any time in the course of a year – should be financed in some other way. One of the most common mistakes made in financing small business, after getting the overall gearing (loans to equity) too high, is relying too heavily on short-term credit. This pushes up the overdraft and extends creditors to such a level that all flexibility is lost.

Government schemes

Government grants tend to be associated with assisted areas, areas of economic deprivation and so on. 'Why go to the middle of nowhere when you can come to the middle of London?' asks the London Docklands Development Corporation.

The whole emphasis of government aid for industry has changed, and at times the scale of aid is not always appreciated. A government moratorium in 1985 placed new emphasis on a number of government aid policies. But this policy is designed in part to put greater emphasis on job creation and to improve cost-effectiveness. The assisted areas, as announced in Parliament on 28 November 1984, are in two tiers: development areas with eligibility for both Regional Development Grants and Regional Selective Assistance, and intermediate areas where only Regional Selective Assistance will be available. Assistance is now being given to services as well as manufacturing industries. Regional Selective Assistance takes two new forms, project grants and in-plant training. Project grants are based on the capital expenditure of the project, and on jobs created or maintained; the first payment being made upon the creation of one third of the jobs and the two remaining payments being made in two instalments, after 12 months and 24 months. The in-plant training scheme requires that the project be located within an assisted area, and that the training is essential to the project's success. Full details are available from the Department of Trade and Industry (see Appendix IV).

At the other end of the scale there is the Enterprise Allowance Scheme, details of which are available from the Department of Employment, through job centres. The main requirements are that you have been unemployed for a minimum of eight weeks and that you have £1,000 capital to put into the company, partnership, co-operative or as a sole trader. Under the scheme an allowance of £40 per week is payable for up to 52 weeks to supplement the income of a new business. But before you decide whether to apply, go and talk to your tax consultant, as certain tax disadvantages might be brought out regarding your own particular situation should you be a sole trader or in a partnership.

Then there is the Loan Guarantee Scheme, which is a form of selective assistance whereby the government guarantees 70 per cent of the loan in order to encourage financial institutions to finance more marginal propositions. The premium of 2.5 per cent for this guarantee is passed on to you, the borrower. This scheme has been revised since its inception and now the borrower has to provide security against the loan. After the 1986 Budget, the LGS was further extended by three years.

Another government scheme, available through the Department of Trade and Industry (previously the BOTB), is that of part-contribution towards the cost of export market research. For companies, the contribution can be up to one third; for groups of two or more unconnected firms participating in joint research, up to a half; and for trade associations up to two-thirds. Also available are loans of up to 50 per cent (up to £300,000) to help set up an overseas operation (Market Entry Guarantee Scheme).

An assistance package was recently launched by the government in conjunction with the EEC, which operates in the most hard-hit areas: steel, shipbuilding and textiles. In England these areas are situated in the North West, North East, Yorkshire and Humberside, and Corby in Northamptonshire. This service applies to a wide range of small firms and is designed not only to encourage business start-ups but also to raise the efficiency of small businesses already trading. Grants are quite wide-ranging and include marketing services (55 per cent grant up to a maximum of £1,500), market research (70 per cent up to a maximum for overseas of £7,000 and domestic £3,500), and management and financial assistance (55 per cent up to a maximum of £2,500). Applications and further details are available through the Department of Trade and Industry regional offices (see Appendix IV).

Another source of finance can be obtained at interest rates well below market. These loans are available from 3i (see address in Appendix IV), using funds provided by the European Coal and Steel Community (ECSC). Primarily, these loans are for existing manufacturing companies although certain service businesses may also qualify. The aim of the project is to create jobs in areas where high unemployment has occurred in the steel and coal industry. Briefly, the loans must be secured by a bank guarantee or equivalent security. 'An ECSC loan can represent up to 50 per cent of the fixed asset

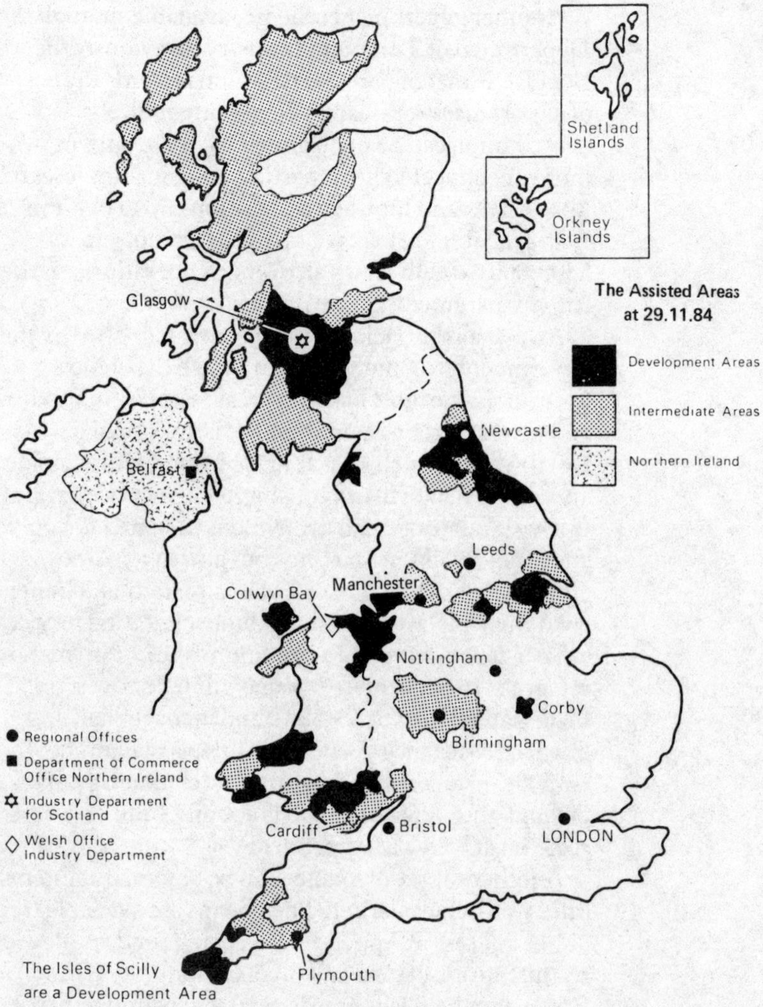

Map of assisted areas in Great Britain

element of the project. There is an upper limit per project of £5 million. Loans are for an eight year period with repayments generally in four annual instalments, starting in the fifth year of the loan. When applying, 3i ask for a full business plan – including five years' historic accounts – together with a profit and cash flow forecasts.'

Enterprise Zones

These zones were set up to encourage the private sector and to benefit the businesses located within the zones by the removal of certain tax burdens such as rates on industrial/commercial property and the relaxation of certain statutory controls. There are 28 sites in all: 19 in England, four in Scotland, two in Northern Ireland and three in Wales. The benefits are available for a 10-year period from the date of the zones' designation. Contact the Department of the Environment for further details (see Appendix IV, Enterprise Zones).

Additional schemes for employing and training people include the Youth Training Scheme, and Computer Skills Training. There are also Energy Efficiency Schemes, and finance is available for technological development through the British Technology Group (formed from the National Enterprise Board and National Research Development Corporation). As government incentives and grants are numerous and can appear confusing to the layman, it is advisable to discuss matters with your local Small Firms Service.

Conclusion

There is a plethora of types of capital for small businesses, and all too often the wrong approach is used in the search for finance – to attempt to raise as much loan finance as possible with minimal personal commitment. The banks and the institutions know by experience that a high proportion of new businesses fail quickly and that most businesses will need more funds than the entrepreneur asks for. It is therefore wise to set out to find the right capital structure; recent government measures have made investments by outside individuals in small firms very attractive. Once you have decided upon the right type of capital which is available to meet your requirements, the next chapter shows you how to present your case to obtain it. Having received some form of finance, we will then show you the sort of records you need to keep and how to monitor and control your business.

2 Presenting your case for raising capital

There are many reasons why you may be wanting to raise capital. If your business is just starting up, or has not been going very long, then you will need to make a presentation for venture capital, possibly to private investors known to you, or to institutional investors who are actively interested in helping to finance the very small business which needs an injection of equity and long-term capital. Or we might be talking about development capital, project capital, or a geared package of equity and loan capital to help in the acquisition of an existing successful business. We could be talking about negotiating a management buy-out, or about exploiting the Unlisted Securities Market (USM) or the Over-the-Counter Market (OTC). Finally, we might be presenting a carefully argued case for UK government or EEC finance. In all these examples we are talking about making a presentation. Whatever your specific case, this chapter covers the general principles you need to know for making a presentation about your company.

How much capital is required?

A healthy profit forecast does not necessarily mean that little capital will be required. Some of the biggest demands on capital are:

— Launching and other preliminary expenses;

— The cost of equipment and premises (sometimes including a premium on leasehold premises);
— The cost of financing stock, work-in-progress and debtors, after allowing for credit granted by suppliers ('working capital');
— Sales falling significantly short of expectations, and other deviations from the original plan.

A word of warning when preparing the budget. There is always the risk that sales will be slow to reach expectations, or even that they will not reach them at all. It is therefore important to make sure that adequate capital is available to cover any reasonable shortfall in profits, and it is strongly recommended that profit and cash projections are prepared to reflect the worst envisaged sales income as well as the most likely sales income. An increase in your sales also has to be financed as it means, for example, that you will have to purchase more raw material; you will also have an increased wage bill, as well as other extra costs.

In your cash forecast you should be prepared to include items where sums for goods are actually received or paid for in cash. These forecasts should be over a two or three-year period, including contingencies, and should show monthly movements, profit/loss and a balance sheet. 'Capital' items such as equipment and leases as well as pre-trading expenditure must also be included. Listed below are items which have a significant impact on cash forecasts and should therefore be borne in mind:

— The proportion of sales expected to be settled in cash rather than by credit;
— The terms of credit, affecting both purchases and sales;
— Staffing levels and the timing of changes;
— Upgrading of accommodation or equipment as the business expands;
— The nature of timing of capital injections.

The cash forecast should cover the same period as the

profit projection, showing projected monthly movements for the first year. It will give you an indication of:

— The maximum capital requirement (before allowing for interest, which will be dictated by the type of financing deal eventually negotiated);
— The month in which the maximum requirement will arise;
— The pattern of the capital requirement (useful to establish the timing of injections and repayments of capital, and the form of finance most suitable);
— The impact on the capital requirement of slower than expected sales progress.

What is the capital required for?
If the evidence gained from your forecasts suggests that much of the capital will be invested in assets on a medium to long-term basis (say, for at least two years), then short-term sources of capital such as a bank overdraft or a temporary loan should not be considered. The components of the capital requirement should be analysed to establish what the fund will be used for and therefore the timescale of the financing required. As a general rule it is best to consider longer-term capital unless dealing with, for example, a business requiring virtually no investment in fixed assets (i.e. equipment and premises), and only reasonable finance for working capital.

Your end objective – a bankable proposition
Most businesses ultimately survive, or not, on the strength of the continuing confidence of their bankers. All other financial dealings must result in a bankable balance sheet. If you insist on proceeding against the better judgement of your bank manager, you will edge your business that much closer to the appointment of a receiver.

The funding of the business should be sufficient and stable enough to enable it to survive a conceivable period of misfortune. Until that position is reached the business will be fragile, and investors and bankers are likely to take a cautious view. Expansion will certainly require finance for more working capital; so will misfortune. Without an adequate equity base you may have no room for manoeuvre.

Seeing it from the other side

This is all about seeing ourselves as others see us, such as bankers and investors. It is often extremely difficult for the smaller businessman to do that; he is sure he is right – and very often he is – but he is not going to convince anyone by assertions. This is where your accountant comes in. He can help you get an objective view of yourself and your business and should be the person who understands what you are currently engaged in. The first point is: *never mind how you see it; present your business as others want to see it*. To do that you are going to have to anticipate your needs: *anticipation* and *control* should be the two themes of your presentation. What a banker appreciates is an application which anticipates what might happen, both the worst and the best, and what you plan to do about it. Your anticipation and contingency planning mean that your management ability will be reflected in the financial picture of the report. A potential backer will also need full details of the business, from machinery to personnel to sales potential. Make sure that all this information is in a readable form.

Have you got a balanced management structure?

Before we discuss the finance of your prospective business in detail, we need to take a look at the management, i.e. you and your partners. The question to ask yourself is whether you and/or your partners or fellow directors have the necessary management expertise for running a business of the kind you hope to start. Take a good look at the experience you can offer between you, and ask yourself whether it is relevant to your proposal. Remember, others will ask these questions about you.

Many small businesses fall into the trap of doing their own projections, which turn out to be wildly optimistic and even dangerous nonsense, leading them to raise too little money for too short a term.

Making an effective proposal

The picture you must present is of the whole business, warts and all. The points which need to be included in any proposal are listed below:

— Description: physical factors, a broad picture of its operation, factors which might strain, limit or influence operations (e.g. space, plant and machinery, trained personnel);
— Its market and its place in that market, even for a corner shop;
— Its base maintainable performance: the level of activity above which you hope to rise but below which there is a very limited danger that you will fall;
— Its track record: trading, not statutory, accounts;
— What factors affect trading, and how;
— Management's ability and credentials.

Put the detail in schedules or appendices so that the opening is brief, and simply portrays the present business. Always remember to set out just the important factors at the beginning. These two maxims are worth remembering: first, *attention starts to wander after four pages*, and secondly, *you may not be there in person to add your explanations*. Your proposal may have to live and fight alone at some area office or bank committee meeting. If you discover that your bank manager will be passing on your proposal to someone else to deal with, find out who it will go to and send it to him yourself.

Sound business

Your banker is going to want to know some very simple things, such as – is the business sound? It is, therefore, important that you really substantiate your base maintainable profit.

Present your case as others will want to see it, and unless you have financial training and are skilled at financial presentations, turn to your accountant to present an objective case. Take a critical look at your business and its future, just as the banker will do. How much? How long? What if? How do I get it back? These are the questions he will want answered. Your presentation should be lucid, logical and frank.

Making assumptions for the future

You should follow your description of the proposition with a careful analysis of the assumptions for the future. Your case is made or broken on the validity of your assumptions and their root in practical business probability. It is vital to get a grip on the essential assumptions about your business, and then put the essence of them across succinctly to your bankers. If they do not understand from your presentation what it is that is crucial to the success or failure of your proposal, and why and how that success or failure comes about, then you will have failed. 'When in doubt do nought' is a banker's motto. Do not blame him – blame your presentation.

One can say, cynically, that your crucial assumptions will be those very reasons you will give as excuses when the project collapses; continuing economic recession, poor market launch, high rates of interest, high wage inflation, lack of skilled labour, cheap imports. All the things which made it not your fault that the project collapsed are the things which should have been properly tackled in your initial assumptions. Some areas for assumptions are:

— The economy of the country;
— Volume of trade: your market;
— Seasonality;
— Personnel;
— Fixed assets and capacity;

— Inflation;
— The competition;
— Pricing;
— Conclusions from market research;
— Interest rates.

Volume of trade is very important. If you want to start a corner shop it is almost impossible to know how many people are going to come in and buy Mars bars. If you are setting up a new factory, it is very difficult to say what the volume of business going through that factory will be. But in both cases you can make a reasonable attempt. You need not go for full-blown market research, but you can ask your professional advisers to take a few perspectives and you can look up some government statistics. Bankers are all too familiar with volume predictions of the type that say 'one item will be sold in the first month, two in the second', and so on. Be realistic; you understand your business and you must convey that confidence and knowledge to the bank.

Your forecasts

The working schedules at the back of your presentation are its engine-room. Here you will have to set out three essential schedules with supporting working papers, which stretch forward over the duration (recommended two to three-year period) of the required finance:

1. Profit and loss: split between the composition of trading gross profit and overheads.
2. Cash flow: showing the contribution from trading before finance, and capital items separately.
3. Balance sheets: including leased assets and leasing liabilities.

Make it clear how the forecasts were arrived at. The assumptions should flow naturally into the profit projections. Some further analysis will help your lender with the answer to 'What if?' Any reader of your presentation should be able to import an assumption of his own and form a view of the impact of that on your business – where, how and with what consequence.

Knowing your business

It is worth pausing here to see what it is that the banker or investor is expecting from the presentation that you have prepared so far. He wants to understand your business, but he also wants to see that *you understand your business*. Most small businesses are too busy running their concerns and pursuing new ideas either to notice what is happening or to explain objectively what it is they have done and what it is they are really going to do. Your lender will also be looking for evidence of competent financial control – evidence that you are where you are knowingly. Many firms believe that any form of planning is a waste of time, but cash forecasting and the discipline of matching plans to resources do not have to be elaborate and are never really wasted. Finally, your lender will be interested in three particular banking concepts: matching finance to its use, gearing and security. All three should be considered together.

Matching finance

When putting together a presentation it is very important not to be tempted to leave the business that you know about and start playing in the business of money. The most common mistake is to attempt to finance long-term assets with short-term money, and to argue that increasing property values are going to make an otherwise not very sensible level of borrowing turn into a profitable venture for you.

Any accountant worth his salt keeps in touch with the banks and the lending institutions and has a feel for the way they are thinking. One of the things that your accountant should do, apart from converting your 'back of the envelope' ideas into an effective presentation, is to insist that your presentation brings out the financial stability which follows from your proposals. Broadly speaking, this means that long-term investment should be funded with long-term money, and readily leasable assets can often be leased at attractive interest rates and over most of their useful lives. Finance for a particular project or asset should be repaid out of the proceeds generated by the business on that project or asset. Do not try to finance one project by the proceeds of another; the road to hell is paved with plans for cross-funding. Overdrafts should be limited to working capital requirements, and should be self-liquidating as part of the trading cycle. The cash-flow and profitability projection should be carried forward so that it can be demonstrated that debt finance is repaid out of cash generated by the project. If that cannot be done, then you probably ought to look for longer-term institutional money.

Gearing

The banker will be interested in two forms of gearing. First, he is concerned about the gearing that emerges from your balance sheet. In the past a banker's norm has been one-to-one capital gearing; in other words, he puts in a pound for every pound you either put in originally or have retained in the business. (Bankers will often say that they prefer this 1:1 gearing ratio; a climb past a 2:1 is often indicative of a banker's concern, in direct proportion to the extent of the climb.) The ideal approach is to demonstrate that even a higher level of gearing initially will correct itself back to a comfortable norm, without relying on crocks of gold.

Secondly, he is interested in income gearing. It shows to what extent the cash flow of the business (generally, profits plus depreciation – that is, cash from trading) covers the repayment of finance, interest and leasing costs.

Security

The banker is also interested in security, but he is much more interested in minimising the risk than in realising his security. Trying to realise a second charge or second mortgage is fraught with problems. No banker wants this type of situation to arise. He is much more interested in the proposition which indicates to him that there is very little risk; after all, bankers do not like putting receivers in or ending up with fleets of tankers or corner shops.

Forecasting for the future

Here you have a choice: you can forecast in 'current-year' pounds, or you can forecast in 'inflated' pounds. If you use the former method – which is preferred by some people working on very large projects – you have a series of inflation differentials that are shown in a curious way, since they are real rate differences expressed in today's money. If you choose the latter method, you take inflation as one of your assumptions and take a view of wage increases and cost increases, and set all these out quite clearly.

A more complex matter is how you predict interest rates. Nobody understands the future, so perhaps you should work in inflated pounds and take a cautious view of declining interest rates.

Finally, it is amazing how many people put forward projections in which they have wholly overlooked some physical bottleneck or some manual or executive difficulty in actually getting that volume of activity to the timescale. Negotiations either with labour forces or with central or local government are in the forefront of such problems.

Finding the right finance

Chapter 1 has guided you through some of the different types of capital available, and this section aims to emphasise the importance of selecting the right kind of finance, and to help you to do this successfully.

For the smaller business, directors' guarantees – usually supported by a charge over personal assets – are generally called for. The banks consider such guarantees necessary because the directors have all the assets under their effective control and the bank wishes to see that the management is totally committed. As to the security offered by the business, you might find that you could borrow up to 80 per cent of property valuations – depending on the location and the economic climate. Debtors can be factored, but a bank will go most of the way to meeting working capital, so long as the overdraft is covered by stocks and debtors by something like one and a half times.

The longer the term of finance you require, the more expensive the presentation. This is because the medium-term assumptions become more and more important and there is more to build on any established track record. Once you are asking for an element of share capital then you are getting close to putting together a prospectus on your business. It is worth stressing here that a viable project with good management does not necessarily succeed in raising finance. It has become accepted that the trouble with this country is that the banks are too unimaginative and our financial institutions too rigid and dominated by security for business proposals to get off the ground. Traditional bank finance in this country does tend to be in insufficient supply in the long term. However, considerable finance is available and is keenly seeking good projects, acquisitions, ventures and buy-outs in which to invest. Recent government budgets ought to mean even more sources of money looking for viable small businesses in which to invest.

It is rarely impossible for a proprietor to raise a modest stake himself. However, you should be aware of the increasing possibility of raising proprietors' equity, and the tax attraction of investment by relatives and friends using the Business Expansion Scheme.

This section is by no means definitive as there are other ways of raising capital. As we have stressed many times before, unless you are familiar with financial arrangement and control, get yourself a good accountant. After all, he is not only qualified to deal with such matters, but he should also be fully aware of the opportunities which are available.

Shopping around

In the case of long-term finance you are bound to find that not only will you have to talk about your proposal several times, but that it is also a good idea to arrange a tour of your operation and management for prospective financial backers. If substantial development capital is required, you may well find that the lender, who is effectively becoming the investor, would like some say in the management of your business, usually by representation on the board. Then, of course, you really must shop around. Money is available just like any other commodity. Different people place different prices on the money they have to offer – dramatically so, when looking for leasing quotes. You must shop around not only amongst lenders of the same type of finance but also between different types of capital. It is nearly always worth getting an opinion from one of the clearing banks – from a lively, enterprising manager local to your business. Sometimes you can go the whole way with a clearing bank; sometimes you will need to move on to a development capital house, venture capital or various institutions. You need to know which corner of the bazaar to visit, and then shop around. You should not overlook government sources of finance – either from central government or from Europe, or, increasingly, from local government.

So there are seven vital factors for small business to remember:

— Prove the volume of business;
— Present the case for others to understand;
— Concentrate on your assumptions;
— Work through a profit and loss and cash flow;
— Provide a series of projected balance sheets;
— Match the assets and finance you are seeking;
— Monitor your business.

Keeping informed

Although not strictly part of any discussion about raising capital, installing and regularly reviewing your financial and management information system is not only important for running a business competently, but it is also an important aspect of raising capital. Any banker will be delighted to find that you have a management information system which will regularly produce monthly accounts comparing your actual performance with your budgeted performance. Your bank manager will be very interested in a simple monthly package for management and for him. This can readily be handled on a micro-computer; but shop around for a good computer package. Accountants have made much more money sorting out off-the-shelf systems which do not work properly than in selling their own.

Cash crises

It is relatively rare that one can be relaxed about cash crises, and these crises can happen whenever a business is thinly capitalised and expanding quickly. There is only a thin line between expansion and over-trading, and over-trading in a business with narrow margins during a time of high interest rates can sometimes tip the scales on a thinly capitalised operation towards a crisis situation.

It is important to realise that cash crises often have nothing to do with profitability. It is a not uncommon mistake for entrepreneurs to wave their internal accounts demonstrating that production is profitable, while simultaneously failing to see that a lot of the profit is going into stock and that the business is not generating cash.

There is, of course, no substitute for anticipation, so your management information system must be cash-sensitive. That should, in turn, imply that your operations are analysed by product, or outlet, or whatever other flow makes up your business, so that you can identify where the money is made or lost and what it is that contributes most to your costs. It is surprising how few businesses know which decisions involving allocation of resources generate cash and which lose cash. It is, however, a medium-term problem to get decision-making right. The short-term solutions are usually to restrict stocks, to work vigorously on debtors, and to defer maintenance and asset purchase either by leasing or renting, or just by ceasing to buy plant and vehicles. Such an organised reduction in the level of activity needs to be handled very carefully. With skill, it can sometimes be achieved with judicious pricing-up. A slightly expensive but perhaps effective proposition might be to factor debts.

Whatever you do, do not tackle the problem of a cash crisis in a piecemeal fashion. It is just as important to present to yourself, to your fellow managers and, maybe inevitably, to your existing or new financial backers, a well-reasoned plan, another presentation if you like, of the agreed action that you intend to take and of the expected results, and then to monitor its achievement.

Some of the most rewarding work for accountants (and for managers and bankers) arises from 'intensive care work' where, through sitting with the company's management, sometimes over a long period, the accountants regain for them the trust and confidence of their bankers, help them pull the company round and nurse it back to health.

Fudged accounts

All too often accountants investigating a company for a client or an investing organisation come across the statement: 'Of course, we are much more profitable than our accounts show us to be. The directors take out £X0,000 in ways other than remuneration. There are lots of assets worth more than is stated in the accounts.'

With today's tax reliefs and opportunities for tax planning it is quite unnecessary to resort to misleading, if not downright false, accounts in order to fudge your way along. When you *do* need money you will have to rebuild that credibility and trust.

Quotation

Finally, you may have long-term plans for the USM, for placing shares with institutions, or even for a Stock

Exchange listing. You cannot prepare too early if your proposed course includes anything like a prospectus. Your presentation will then start with an accountant's investigation, known as a 'long-form report'. This will include a profit forecast and an examination of working capital needs. These investigations are rigorous, and your sponsors will rely on them. Any broker or issuing house which tells you that they are not needed, or that they can be curtailed, is a sponsor not worth having.

Conclusion

Make sure that you have a brief synopsis of the age, education and experience of yourself and your partners to prove that you are capable of running the business, and remember that in most cases you will not be present when the final decision is made. Make sure too that the assets you and your partner are putting up are shown. Give brief details of your business, the product, its market, the competition; if you are already in business, then show the latest accounts with up-to-date profit and loss as well as borrowing history. Give details of your key personnel, their functions and qualifications, and supply a list of the principal shareholders. Do explain fully the purpose of the business and the market-place in which its products are competing; your presentation will not be complete with just the financial information. Profit projections must be broken down to show costings, project sales, orders held, legal and audit fees. Be factual and state precisely the amount of finance required and what it will be used for, and make sure that your projections include repayments in the cash flow. Lastly, make sure that assets can be held as security – this is your way of saying, 'I know what I am doing and to prove it I am putting up my own money.'

Be prepared, and before deciding who to approach for financial backing, go along and talk it through with your accountant. He will be in the best position to advise you on the different types of finance available and, more importantly, the kind of finance best suited to your needs. Be quite clear as to what your proposal will include and what assets are available for security purposes. Finally, it is worth noting that a presentation made via a professional intermediary (i.e. financial consultant or accountant) is often considered in a more favourable light by potential backers, as such a person is used to making proposals on behalf of others and will be known in your local financial community. Having a presentation done in this way can add great weight to your case.

3 Finding the right premises

'There are three things important in property: location, location and location.' Whatever the size and type of your business, it is vital to have suitable accommodation as well as to be in the right location if you are to run it profitably and efficiently. When looking for accommodation, the main thing is to plan as far as possible in advance. It may be that you have certain timescales laid down for you: your lease may be coming to an end, or you may have a certain piece of plant on order for which there is a delivery date for installation in your new property. Dealing with property is a complex subject and not all the factors will be under your control, so you need to avoid a mad panic in the last few weeks. Whatever business you are starting and whatever your needs, whether it is a corner shop, or an office or a factory, do list precisely what your requirements are before starting your search.

What sort of premises do you need?

Your business may be the sort where the actual dimensions of the building do not matter, where it is simply the square footage that needs to be taken into account. For instance, if you need a racking system in your warehouse, the building may have to be of a specific width and length. Height is also important for warehousing, and for some industrial users. There are many other questions which may need answering:

— Are you going to lease or purchase and what price can you afford?

— Are irregular shapes acceptable, or must it be rectangular or square?
— Can you accept pillars or do you need a clear span?
— Are you going to have your offices and factory in the same complex? Do you need any additional floor space in the foreseeable future?
— Is there sufficient capacity of gas, water, electricity and drainage for your needs?
— How secure should the property be in order to meet your insurance requirements?
— Do you want (and can you afford) a prominent or prestigious building or situation?
— How essential is the accessibility of your suppliers and your own transport?
— If you do have your own transport, are you heavily reliant on it? If not, how accessible are modes of nationalised transport, such as British Rail and National Carriers?
— Do you have any other special requirements specifically related to your business?

Do consider all these factors in advance before approaching either the Council or estate agents.

Buy or lease?

There are three types of property; freehold, ground lease and leasehold, with the first and last being the most popular with small companies and shops setting up. Ground lease is less popular as it means you have to rent the ground and then build your factory, which means that your costs rise. For new businesses, commercial mortgages may be difficult to obtain and therefore close consideration needs to be given to this matter. But if you have been established as a business for some time and if you buy a sound property at the right price, it should become a good capital investment over the years. In the past when you decided to realise your money from the sale of a commercial property, you found that it had been an excellent hedge against inflation. Unfortunately, in many localities throughout the UK, this is not now the case. If your bank manager holds the title deeds, a valuation from a reputable firm of professional valuers will be sufficient for granting an overdraft or a mortgage or another form of advance. Providing that you stay within the statutory law, you can do with a freehold property basically what you will. The problem with buying is having to raise the purchase money. You will also have to be sure that your business can generate enough profit to pay the interest on the loan and it is quite likely that the risk capital you have will give a much greater return if it is employed in the business rather than invested in the property. The level of return expected on premises in the long term is generally much lower than that expected if capital is invested within the business.

One advantage of leasing is that there is no capital outlay in acquiring the building. In general terms, it is just a question of fitting out – which you would have to do anyway with a purchased building. The principle of the Landlord and Tenant Act 1954, together with subsequent amending legislation, is that when your lease comes to an end you have the right to remain in occupation under the terms of a new lease. There are two principal exceptions to this rule. If you have been a bad tenant, then obviously the landlord can get you out. But what is slightly more important as far as the tenant is concerned is that if the landlord wants to occupy his premises for his own purposes, or wants to redevelop, then he can, under certain circumstances, take possession against you. Normally, he will have to pay you compensation on a statutory basis, and this is related to rateable value and the time you have been in possession. However, a tenant usually has restricted freedom of action.

If you lease a building, you will sign a tenancy agreement with your landlord in which he will ensure to the best of his ability that you are covenanted to look after the property and not to make any alterations or change its use without his approval. There will be other restrictions on what you can actually do to property, accompanied by regular rent reviews. Furthermore, you will not build up any equity in the property; in other words, when you come to dispose of your interest you will, at best, get only a nominal value for it unless a clause in your lease permits you to sell your outstanding lease to another.

Do not consider leasing a space larger than required for the purpose of sub-letting. There are strong restrictions on sub-letting and there is the added risk that (in most areas) you may not be able to sub-lease the extra space and you will still have to pay rent, rates, insurance and maintenance on it.

While the landlord has by law to let the property and meet the statutory requirements when leasing the property, it is the lessee's responsibility to ensure that the premises comply with the Health and Safety at Work Act.

Always make sure that you know precisely how much you are paying and what you are getting for that amount; this applies particularly to the service charge.

Charges per square foot for modern industrial property vary but as a rough guide the rent for 1,000 sq ft (not city centre property) can be from £3.50 to £4.75 per sq ft in the Midlands and the North and upwards of £8.50 per sq ft in London. (Prices in the Golden Corridor, situated in the Thames Valley, can be higher still.) The cost of office accommodation also varies, so it is best to talk to a professional who knows the areas in which you are interested.

Most modern industrial buildings are single-storey constructions but older buildings may not be. Consideration as to the floor loading is of particular importance to the industrialist and warehouseman and in view of the new types of office equipment, the loading factor is also becoming important for office users. In older buildings this may present a problem.

Is there sufficient capacity of gas, water, electricity and drainage for your needs? For example, if the building has only a two-inch gas supply and you have ordered a new industrial oven that requires a capacity needing, say, a four-inch supply, then obviously you must calculate the cost of putting in the new gas main before you decide to buy the property. Take a look at the condition of the existing services, especially in an older building. If the main electrical switchgear has been condemned, it can be very costly to renew. If you have a need for special services, such as butane gas, oxygen or compressed air, do ensure that you are able to install these services, both from the physical point of view and also in terms of any permission you may have to obtain from a landlord, local authority or other statutory bodies.

How many car parking spaces will you need both for your employees and for your visitors? Try to ensure that all the vehicle circulation arrangements operate efficiently. Look carefully at transport; the cost of running vehicles today is high and still rising so it is becoming increasingly important to ensure that you can get all your goods in and out as quickly as possible. Calculate the size of vehicles that you anticipate will be arriving at your premises; make sure in advance that they will be able to avoid congestion. Remember too, that vehicles are getting bigger and business requirements may well change, so allow room for expansion.

Do you have any other requirements? For example, if you are in the jewellery business, you will require good natural daylight. What about ventilation and air conditioning? And if you are dealing with valuable materials such as gold or copper, or with confidential documents, then good security will be an important factor. There are two ways of dealing with this. First, consider the building itself; obviously the fewer doors and windows it has in the outside walls the more secure it will be. Secondly, if you wish to install security devices such as electronic beams and a trembler unit, then you have to determine how easily they can be installed. Also, remember that if the building is leased you will require the landlord's approval for these alterations. A precise analysis of your business will also throw up additional needs. An example of this is if you are in a steel-stockholding business, then you will need a crane not only to load and unload the steel, but also to move it within your premises.

Where do I begin?

Contact the employment promotion units run by local authorities and government agencies. You will find them in the local telephone directory and they are extremely helpful in giving details of premises. Other government authorities will also be very helpful. If you want a rural location, speak to the Rural Development Commission, previously CoSIRA (the Council for Small Industries in Rural Areas). The best way of locating the government agency best suited to help you is to contact the Small Firms Centre of the Department of Employment. There are a number of offices scattered throughout the country, and if you ask for Freefone 'Enterprise' the operator will put you in touch with the nearest office.

The vast majority of properties on the market are advertised, so the columns of your local newspaper will also give you a good idea of what is available. If not it may be worthwhile to place your own advertisement in the 'premises wanted' column. It is also useful to drive around the desired areas and see what you can find, not only from the point of viewing suitable property but also to see if any of your competitors are in the immediate area.

Chartered surveyors and estate agents

If you feel that you need professional assistance then you should contact either a chartered surveyor or an estate agent. There are a number of firms, both large and small, in most towns and cities which deal with the selling and leasing of commercial and industrial property, offices and shop premises; you will find them listed in the local directories. Find out what service each one can offer and under what terms. Take advice from colleagues with a personal knowledge of the various firms and then choose the surveyor or agent who is best suited to your purposes. Brief him about the type of property you require and your price range. He will know what is available in the market and at what price.

As he is acting on your behalf it will be the estate agent's job to negotiate the best terms for you. However, it is as well to keep yourself informed as to how matters are progressing. Town planning matters, rating and insurance valuations are also dealt with by him. If you need to raise a mortgage or loan for the acquisition of the property then the agent can do the valuation for you. If you are considering development, then planning permission is required and building regulation approval gained; after that the council controls the standard of building. And this is where the chartered surveyor plays a key role. If you have a property to sell, the estate agent can advise you on the best method of marketing it, the price to ask, and he can also put it on the market and negotiate the sale. In any case it is advisable to get an independent opinion from a surveyor when purchasing or leasing your chosen property. Your solicitor will scrutinise the terms of lease or purchase before you sign.

New or existing premises?

If you are an exporter, you may feel that when your foreign buyers come in you will want to show them a modern, clean-looking, efficient property. If you renovate or store machinery you may be able to make do with something less impressive. These are only two of the considerations when deciding on new or existing premises.

One advantage of new premises is lower repair and maintenance costs. If the building has been designed correctly and built to the proper standard then it will require very little attention – certainly for the first five or ten years. A new building is more likely to meet modern requirements in terms of thermal insulation, traffic circulation, car-parking provisions and so on.

If the building is specifically designed for your purposes it can incorporate your exact requirements, and still leave room for expansion. The disadvantage of a new building is the higher cost of purchasing and also renting. In addition, the rates on a new building will be relatively higher than on existing premises. And by the time you have gone through planning permission and had the building designed and built, you can easily find that some 12 months or so has passed, even for the most modest scheme – and considerably longer for something more ambitious. If you are in a hurry this sort of timescale may not be acceptable.

An advantage of existing buildings is their availability. The number of new buildings on the market at any one time will obviously be far less than the number of existing buildings, and therefore there is a much greater choice. Existing buildings are also cheaper although they will have higher maintenance and running costs. It should also be remembered that adaptation costs can be surprisingly high if the building has to be altered to suit your business needs – even the most minor work can cost several thousand pounds. Moreover, a building that was put up in the 1950s almost certainly will have no thermal insulation to speak of, and so your heating bills are going to be higher than in a modern building.

Fire officers, health and safety executives, and factory inspectors, are becoming stricter all the time. What was acceptable ten years ago will not be passed today, and you may well be obliged to carry out certain improvements. There is also the disadvantage that, if the building is old or in a poor location, it may not hold its value as an investment and may be difficult to sell when you move to a more modern or larger property. It is therefore wise to seek professional advice.

Choosing your site

Clearly, you will want to ensure that transport costs are kept to a minimum. Therefore it may well be that by siting your property adjacent to a motorway junction, railway station, harbour or airport, you can considerably improve the efficiency and profitability of your company. If you are starting from scratch, you will obviously want to ensure that you can obtain the right skills in your chosen locality. Contact the Department of Employment as they will have a great deal of information about the skills available in your area. But if you are moving an existing business, then you will want to be sure that all your workers are willing and able to move to your new location. Make sure too that the move will not hinder future sales.

If you find that you buy all your raw materials from one particular source, or that 80 per cent of your goods are delivered to one customer, then obviously this must be a factor to bear in mind when deciding on the location of your premises.

Town planning requirements are particularly important, because the property must have planning permission for the use to which you are going to put it. Look very carefully at any conditions that are attached to the planning permission: for example, there may be noise restrictions or restrictions on working hours, which could present very serious drawbacks. If the property does not have planning permission for your purpose, then discuss the matter with the local town planning officer. If you do not make any progress, then seek professional advice on how to proceed.

Values are particularly important in the case of retail operators. You may decide that you would very much like to be located in the middle of the main shopping street in Birmingham but cannot afford the rent. In this case you may have to seek the next best thing: an area where the levels of rent are within your grasp which is still in an acceptable trading location.

Many new small businesses will be owner/occupier. Although not necessarily an investment – the prime concern is running a business – if you buy a property you will have committed a considerable amount of effort and possibly money, and therefore it is wise to ensure that when you do sell you can get your money back. If you work from home, then you can claim some of your heating and related costs. However, do not forget that you can be subject to capital gains tax if you claim against the rates. Be sure to take reliable professional advice on this.

If you are moving to a new area in order to set up business and will be looking for a separate house then you will probably want to look for the best you can afford. If you have children to educate, then obviously you will want to make sure that they go to good schools. If you do not want to do too much travelling, you will want to be satisfied that the local public transport is accessible and that the distances you will have to cover are reasonable.

You may be quite happy to operate next door to or close by one of your competitors because you think you are twice as good as he is. But a lot of people take the view that they do not want to be too near people in the same line of business – the rule here should be to make sure that you are aware of the location of any competition before you move. Grants are available from many local authorities who are anxious to encourage new businesses. (Contact 3i, see Appendix IV.) However, at the time of writing, the government no longer offers an exchange risk guarantee cover which was an important factor as the loans are available in European currencies. Necessary cover against currency fluctuations should be taken into account if considering these loans. In the assisted areas (see map page 32) there are substantial grants to encourage you to locate your business there. Telephone your local Department of the Environment for details (see Contact points on page 213).

If you have, or are thinking of setting up, a hi-tech business, then there are a growing number of Science or Business Parks being built throughout the country. These parks are a relatively new inclusion in Britain and the units are specially designed to assist the new small business, treating it as an embryo unit. Common facilities, such as managerial assistance, administration and secretarial work are usually included in the package. In addition to time-sharing facilities there are other benefits, such as published research, technological expertise, and shared expenses on expensive equipment.

There are also Enterprise Zones (see Chapter 1 and Appendix IV) as well as Special Development and Development Areas. Widespread assistance is available in these areas in the form of incentives, mainly financial. Again, information can be obtained from the local offices of the Department of the Environment.

Freeports have also been established and are located in areas of high unemployment in order to assist in the creation of new jobs. There are many Freeport Zones internationally, but in Britain they are a new idea and will have to prove themselves in less than five years. Basically, they are small secured areas where duty does not have to be paid on imported goods until it crosses the Freeport boundary, and it does not have to be paid on goods re-exported. There are many advantages in locating a business in a Freeport although the two major disadvantages to be borne in mind are the cost of premises and the time-factor, as mentioned above.

Finally, before you decide to move into your new premises – having already calculated in advance all the costs of agent's fees as well as solicitors' and other professional fees, petrol, telephoning, removal and time – look around you. Have you considered equipment? How are you going to pay for the furniture and stationery? Have you thought of the cost of getting your letterheads printed? Though you will be able to claim allowances for many of these items, make sure that you have planned for this extra cost in your budgets.

4 Marketing and sales

Marketing is a 'creative management function which promotes business and employment by assessing needs of the end-user of products or services, initiates research and development, and produces products and services which can be profitably provided to satisfy market requirements. It co-ordinates the resources of production and distribution of goods and services, determines and directs the nature and scale of the total effort required to sell profitably the maximum production to the ultimate user.' (Source: *International Dictionary of Management*.) This statement clearly defines the concept of marketing to present your company's products and services to the customers. This awareness of the necessity for marketing has grown increasingly over the last 20 years as companies, both large and small, seek to survive in a more challenging and competitive business world. Marketing and sales must work together to achieve the end result of increased sales and to co-ordinate and put into action the overall policies of the company.

Marketing covers a wide spectrum, from research design and product development through packaging, public relations and promotion to sales and after-sales service. It is both for internal and external benefit and information. It is the total approach as well as the presentation which ensures the profitable running of the business. Marketing enables the company to supply what the customer wants, while selling ensures that the customer buys what the company offers.

You should not become complacent just because you have a product that sells, and you are making a profit. The key to success lies in analysing your product/service to find out your strengths and weaknesses and to act accordingly.

It is a false assumption that marketing means spending a lot of money; this need not be the case – although as with everything you will need a budget.

First, let us examine the 'marketing mix'. Be honest with yourself and answer these questions fully:

1. What sector of the market do your clients come from and who are they?
2. When and why do they buy your product?
3. Are they end-users or do they in turn sell to someone else?
4. Who are your competitors and what is your share of the market?
5. How do your competitors market their product and do you know their success rate?
6. Has your market-place changed over the last few years?
7. What sells your product – is it the price, the packaging, the product or the advertising? (Your answer to the last question should be all four points. If sales success is based solely on price then you leave yourself open to price cutting by your competitors. If it is based on the product itself, your competitors can in time supply an almost identical product.)
8. How do we – the company – sell our product?
9. Do I need to alter my product (or service) to increase my sales? If so, how?
10. Is there any other cost-effective product or service which is a natural 'spin-off' from my present product(s)/service(s) that I can offer?

Marketing is a combination of a number of aspects all aimed at a 'customer-first' policy, and can succeed only if there is total commitment not only from the board of directors/owners and managers but also from the staff.

The continued motivation of staff is a key area and not one to be overlooked. If your staff is not well motivated, then your marketing policy will count for nothing.

We must analyse ourselves and our product; we must be totally committed to marketing and selling our product; we must know it thoroughly so that we can present it to its best possible advantage not only in sales but in advertising, packaging and promotion. But how do we build it into our firm? We cannot afford to hire a whizz kid! In small companies marketing can be handled by the managing director or sales director, but as the company grows then it will need outside expertise, either in the form of a consultant or a new employee, assuming that an employee has not been trained to take over this function.

Marketing must have clear and well-defined objectives and methods to improve a business's products but above all it needs management, and organisation now becomes the key word. The marketing methods used should be geared to the customer and must be flexible and competitive. They must also take into account the image of the firm that you want to project. Being all things to all men is difficult, if not impossible, but a marketing man must have sufficient creativity to overcome diverse problems.

Now that you have answered all the questions, you will need to sit down and produce a marketing budget to include promotional literature, direct mailings, advertising if necessary, and your sales targets, as these will need to be taken into consideration. Just as it is wrong to assume that you need to spend vast sums of money on marketing, it is also a fallacy to believe that you can market properly by not spending any money; you cannot gain your marketing goals without spending a certain amount. The best thing to do is to create a budget and work within it.

But how do we promote our product? There are no hard and fast rules which state that your product must be sold or marketed in a certain way and this is why your market research and analysis can be so critical. As time goes by they will become more refined, but it is important to remember that each marketing discipline must follow closely the facts gained from them.

Market research

There are many companies you can employ to get answers to your market research questions. However, if your budget is small, you could try collection, collation and analysis of information yourself, providing you are clear about the information you seek. Have you already done a trial study? If not, you should.

There is plenty of information available; it is a question of tapping the source, and it is here that your sales staff can help as they have constant contact with the customers. This personal knowledge is very important. But as with everything, the information-gathering programme needs to be defined according to the information you already have, and the information you still need. Moreover, sources and their value will vary and must be taken into account when compiling your questionnaire. You must also know the key groups of customers and be able to identify their answers. The important thing is to keep your questions simple and straightforward and not to make it sound as if you are playing 'Twenty Questions'. Do not alter the questions' content during the course of the market research programme as this will affect your analysis. One of the most effective ways of conducting market research is by using the telephone, but you can also use the post, personal interviews or direct observations.

The market research programme must be properly controlled and much time will be spent on organising it, which on occasions may seem to be a waste of time and money. However, without such a programme you have no base of knowledge of your market-place; it could, moreover, identify gaps in your product range which in turn could generate new ideas or products.

Advertising

Advertising is a multi-media operation which takes many forms, ranging from commercial TV and radio to advertising in national or local newspapers, trade and technical magazines. Some of these will obviously not be of any use to you, due to the cost of the product or the size of your company. Whichever form of advertising is used, as long as it is successfully targeted, it can reach potential customers who in turn can become clients. But do not commit yourself to advertising before you have studied the market you are aiming at and the media involved in that market. Go to your local library and look at a copy of BRAD (British Rate and Data) and you will find the different types of magazines, newspapers, etc. For example, if you are selling second-hand luxury cars then you could consider placing an advertisement in *Exchange & Mart* or *Autocar* as by doing this you are advertising in a medium which is most frequently read by car enthusiasts and they are your potential sales market.

When you 'rough-out' your advertisement you need to remember that you are informing people, stimulating interest and prompting action; point out the benefits to the reader rather than just blandly putting information on a sheet of paper. As there will be other advertisements on the page you will need to grab the reader's attention, so do not clutter the advertisement with unintelligible jargon unless you are sure that your target market will fully understand it. Pay close attention to the design of your advertisement.

Again, you will need a budget, as you should be planning your advertising as part of an overall campaign. Costing will be very important. However, bear in mind that whether you use an agency or place advertisements yourself, you get a reduction per insertion depending on the number of bookings (insertions) placed. Each magazine/paper produces its own rate card, readership records, etc., so do ask for one. Also, check the level of responses to your advertisements and remember that the true cost is in reaching your potential customer.

Public relations

Often called the best means of advertising, public relations plays a very important part in any business's marketing process; not only is it cheaper than its other marketing colleagues but it also packs far more punch, because at its heart lies an independent opinion.

The businessman in the first instance has to overcome his reservations about the media and in the second instance, he must realise that his firm can be newsworthy in the eyes of the media corps. All forms of media are always looking for stories of interest or success, and if yours is sufficiently interesting and is made available to them, there is every chance of getting it broadcast or printed. To arrange all your public relations, do not forget to include both local and national newspapers, magazines, local as well as regional and national radio stations and, of course, television companies. However, before you make any contact, you must devise an effective public relations campaign. There are many public relations consultants to choose from, should you not want to undertake the task yourself. Ensure that you know what you want from the campaign, what you are going to put across, and the market area you want this information to go to. Then you can decide how to put it across and which media to use. There is another point to remember, however: it is very difficult to assess in monetary terms the success of your campaign; a simple costing of expenditure versus sales cannot produce an overall picture showing the success rate of your campaign.

The simplest way of getting your point across in a public relations campaign is to issue press releases. It is worth printing letterheads with the words 'Press Release' across one corner or centred in the middle of the sheet. When writing a press release, make sure that you have a 'punchy' headline. Many press releases will be put in front of the editor and only the ones that catch his eye will be pulled out to read. The text should be brief and explain precisely the point you wish to put across, and it must keep the reader's interest. Keep the release to one (maximum two) A4 pages with double line spacing. Paragraphs should be kept short. Do not forget to put the name of your business, its address and telephone number and a contact name for further information at the end of each release. If you have a relevant photograph, include that as well.

An effective public relations campaign can do your firm a lot of good. The key point is to build up a good rapport with your local newspapers and radio stations.

Direct mail

An increasingly popular and cost-effective way of selling your product is using direct mail: direct mailing has undergone something of a revolution in recent years, but it can also be the source of a lot of wasted energy and money.

Direct mail relies on three factors:

1. The mailing list, its accuracy and target potential.
2. The product on offer, its desirability and price.
3. The sales impact of the direct mail copy and ease of sales.

The first question often asked is: where do I begin? You can start to collect your own circulation list from market research, existing clients and advertising responses; or, if you wish to go about it more quickly, direct mail (or marketing) consultants can help by supplying the lists and giving advice. If you are 'testing the water' then speak to the marketing department of the Post Office as they offer special mailings for first-time users.

Careful selection of your list is very important as it directly affects your response rate. Consider the size of your mailing too: ask yourself whether your business can cope with the direct mail campaign itself and a high response rate.

There are certain rules to adhere to when writing

copy for direct mailers. The first is to test the mailer's effectiveness before having it printed. The second priority must be to ensure that it is sent to the *decision-maker*, the person who will be buying your product. Below are six further points to bear in mind:

1. Keep the mailer's copy short, direct and, above all, *accurate*. Avoid putting too much text down as you want to keep the reader's attention. You are not writing a story, you are selling your product.
2. Make sure that you do not swamp the recipient with a mass of literature – it can be very offputting to receive a lot of separate items in one envelope.
3. Try to send each mailing in a white envelope rather than a brown one. The presentation has a better appearance although it is more expensive. Remember, the envelope can also be used as part of the overall campaign.
4. Make sure that your mailer makes it easy for potential clients to reply. Special offers and free samples can be used.
5. Send a letter with the mailer and always make it personal.
6. Depending on the volume and on whether you can afford the cost, try to use at least two-colour printing for the mailer.

When you receive your replies, assess your response rate and monitor the sales. If necessary, the copy can then be amended to attract other clients on subsequent mail shots; make sure each different mailer is coded so that monitoring is easy and effective.

Your response rate will not be immediately obvious. Expect the first replies within a two to three-week period with some replies taking six to ten weeks – sometimes even longer. Depending on the size of the mailer, the accuracy of the list, and correct targeting, redemption rates can vary enormously from one quarter of one per cent to seven per cent or more.

Upon receipt of replies, do ensure that each one is dealt with swiftly and professionally by either your sales team or by the relevant customer service person. If further details are required then these must be sent out promptly. There is no point in initiating response if this service is slow off the mark or non-existent.

Other marketing aids

As well as direct mail and advertising, there are many other sales aids which can be developed; these range from offers of free gifts to competition. Check your budget to ensure you can afford this extra expenditure. If you can afford a special offer, then include a reply coupon in your mailer.

Exhibitions and trade shows also play an important part, although costs can be high. Company literature, leaflets and 'point-of-sale' material rely heavily on design and end-use. In each case, when deciding which marketing method to use, you should consider four important factors.

1. The requirements of your business.
2. The current financial situation of business.
3. The cost-effective of each type of campaign.
4. Can your current production output cope with an influx of orders?

Marketing is many things, but common sense, knowledge of the market-place and what it can and cannot take must always be taken into consideration.

Sales

Your sales force is your front line and it is your salesmen's skill that ensures a healthy turnover of contracts. Although this is stating the obvious, no matter how many administrative systems or accounting procedures you have, your company could not exist without sales. Your salesmen must work very closely with the marketing department as both can help each other immeasurably. A salesman is born, not made; selling is a skill. It is a combination of job commitment, product knowledge and the ability to put across the point which tells the client what he wants to hear so that he can buy the product or service on offer. The closing of the sale is as necessary as initiating the contact. This holds true for both on-the-road sales personnel and for telephone sales too (the latter is more cost-effective and can be used with great benefit as a backup or customer supply service).

Many businessmen find it difficult to sell and this comes across to the customer. If you are a sole trader or in a small partnership or company then you will have to train yourself to go out and sell your product – remembering that selling is a two-way communication. But before you go out, consider first what your prime objectives are. Is the achievement to be the making of appointments? Or is it to be the sale? Once you have decided, then motivate yourself into a 'positive-thinking' attitude and keep your objective in mind. This 'positiveness' will come across to the client as knowledge and professionalism and will help you to achieve your goal.

Initiating contact

You may well ask, 'How do I find customers to call on?' The first thing to do is to research and select your market. Keep client cards of all these prospects noting names, addresses, telephone numbers, dates of contacts, results and further details.

Let us assume that your first goal is to make an appointment and your second goal is going to see the prospective client to sell your product or service. This is oversimplifying matters as it may take a number of calls to get through to the right person. However, despite the number of calls you make, try not to be too pushy on the telephone as you will merely irritate the receptionist or secretary and are unlikely to get through. A telephone call ('cold-calling') to these likely clients is the first thing to do in order to ascertain whether you have got in touch with the decision-maker and whether the client is currently buying a similar product or would be interested in making an appointment to see your own product.

Of course, if you have already established contact or if it is an existing client then the approach is different. At this stage you are the best one suited to judge the right level of communication.

If you are given leads always follow them up, either by writing a letter or by telephoning the prospect. Always keep your customers and potential customers happy and 'cared for'. Make sure that your system is geared to deal with such enquiries.

Whatever your level, whether you are a salesperson or running a small sales force, there will always be a number of 'golden rules' which will need to be followed.

— Always ask searching questions to ascertain your clients' (or potential clients') specific needs;
— Listen to the answers to find out what the person really wants;
— Watch out for tell-tale signs of boredom;
— Do not overstay your welcome. Better to make another appointment and come back, keeping your client happy and still looking forward to seeing you again. Some people cannot be rushed into making a decision, and if you do apply pressure, the sale can be lost;
— Keep your goal in mind.

Selling is all about achieving and meeting targets. Therefore, salespeople must either have targets set for them or they must set targets. However, be realistic and do not set targets for either yourself or your sales force which you know cannot be met. Also, do not put pressure on production time or delivery schedules when it is not necessary.

Presentations

Although it has been mentioned before, it is worth stressing that presentations must be prepared prior to the meeting. A professional image must be presented at all times. And, above all, know your product.

A few further 'golden rules' to bear in mind when presenting to clients or speaking to them on the telephone:

— Never promise what you cannot deliver;
— Never let your client see that you have a problem;
— Never be too pushy or aggressive as this can lose a sale;
— Never criticise your competitors – the attitude to take is 'they are good, but we are better' or simply do not mention them;
— Never criticise your colleagues or the business or its product(s);
— Never argue with the client; turn the point around by asking questions.

The main area in which sales are lost in a presentation is in the closing of the sale. Some people are frightened to ask for a commitment and avoid the closing question. Be positive, ask the client: 'When shall we deliver?' 'Do we agree that . . . ?' 'Do I have your approval on . . . ?' 'Do you want it if we can get it?' 'How many would you like?' It is a waste of time to make a presentation, get the client interested and then back away from asking for a commitment at the last moment. The client will not mind being asked.

Conclusion

Salespeople need management, motivation and control; recognition of a job well done develops a sense of achievement. It is relatively easy to see when a salesman is not working well but it is more difficult to find out why. Be sympathetic and try to find out the reasons for the lack of or decrease in sales performance. It is a good idea to have a commission rate system based on performance but at the same time it should be linked to security by the provision of a basic salary. Motivation can also help. A *Daily Telegraph* title in the Business Enterprise Series, *Motivating through Incentives*, is recommended reading as it explains the different areas of motivation, and the possible achievements.

Sales are the life-blood of a business: without the selling of your product, you would not be in business at all.

5 Control and financial management

It has been suggested that the current recession, with its attendant unemployment, is providing the impetus for people to go it alone; but whilst there is scope for growth and development, the risk of failure is very high. So having set out on your own, effective control of your business is vital. Yet so often we find that it is exactly this which is missing. The businessman gets on with what he considers the real work and neglects the controls, and the business suffers accordingly.

Planning

One factor which affects small and large businesses alike is the rate of change. During the last few years we have seen an accelerating rate of change: products are on sale today that were not even thought of ten or even five years ago. In this climate, planning – especially financial planning – is of the utmost importance. The well-managed company needs to be constantly alert to change. The prime questions to ask yourself are:

— Where are we now?
— Where do we want to go?
— What resources (financial and manpower) do we have?
— What is our performance like?
— What are our objectives?

— How are we going to reach them?
— What is holding us back?
— What tactics do we use?
— What is the competition?

Then, as managers, we have to start to make it happen.

Fixing your objectives

Let us start at the beginning. Where do we want to go? Write your objectives down. If you do not know where you want to go, your chances of arriving are not good.

Identifying the constraints
The next step is to ask: What constraints are holding us back? Typically the answers fall into three main areas: finance, management and markets.

1. FINANCE. The worst time to go to your bank and ask to borrow money is when you are in desperate need of it; when this happens it is often the result of poor financial control. Statistics show that 90 per cent of companies go bust within the first ten years, and the level of bankruptcies and liquidations is growing; 90 companies per week in the UK are currently going into liquidation. Most insolvencies can be avoided if the management directs proper attention to cash-flow problems. A major deficiency in small businesses is often a lack of 'information' about the cash requirements. But information concerning what? The answer is: cash flow and profitability.

Financial control involves dealing effectively with each of the individual steps in the cycle:

(a) Having the necessary information to facilitate day-to-day management of the assets and liabilities of the business.
(b) Having the right information to plan the overall cash needs of the business and to evaluate the worth of future projects and alternative proposals.
(c) Having the information needed for measuring actual results and comparing them with the plan.

(d) Having advance information to enable the business to do a proper job of tax planning.

Each business has different financial pressure points, ranging from effective debtor control to seasonal peaks and sudden large payments. It is the gathering of such information that is an important ingredient in solving financial problems.

It is vital to make sure that either you have sufficient cash reserves, or you are able to look ahead to when you may need the money. If you can make a good case for it and show that you have a profitable idea, then often it is not that difficult to raise the money (in which case, it was not really a financial constraint in the first place). Alternatively, when you work the proposal out carefully, it may not look such a good idea after all and you will be unable to raise the money – but in that case it was only because the business plan was faulty in the first place.

2. MANAGEMENT. Starting off in a small business you may not be lucky enough to have any managerial assistance, in which case you have to become a 'jack of all trades'. This situation may not last, however, and once you start to expand, increasing your turnover and the size of your company or business, then you need to consider the extra managerial layer needed – middle management. The first type of management expertise you need may be in the financial and sales/marketing areas. You could find that some of your employees 'in the back room' have hidden talents which could be useful to you. But in any case this is the time when you have to be very careful that your control structure and overheads are in line with your activities.

As your business grows and your middle management expertise needs to be 'bought in', make sure first of all that it cannot be found in existing employees. Consultants can be expensive and selecting those suitable to your business's needs is time-consuming. Before employing a consultant seek recommendations first. Always select a reputable firm and one which has had prior working experience in your field of business. Enquire as to the size of company the firm normally works for. Above all, consider whether you can afford their fees. To some extent these points apply to any external professionals you engage, such as your accountant or solicitor.

As each department is formed, you must be careful that guidelines are laid down so that the workload and personnel supervision are clearly defined. This is often a weak point in medium-sized companies. As your company expands further and you find that you are no longer able to oversee all the departments, the time has come to appoint a general manager.

The management of a business should function as a well-oiled machine and be structured to resemble a pyramid. This pyramid must be watched closely, as if it becomes reversed, this can lead to very serious problems indeed.

Arthur C. Clarke, the science fiction writer, sums it up very nicely: 'The company which concentrates on the present may have no future; in business as in everyday life, wisdom lies in striking a balance between the needs of today and those of tomorrow. It is true that the farmer whose house is on fire must stop the sowing to put out the fire, but he will lose much more than his house if he doesn't prepare for next year's crop.

3. MARKETS. Financial planning is not just looking inwards – it must look outwards as well. One of the hardest things for a small business to do is to keep an eye on what is going on outside. It is very important that you do not lose sight of what is happening around you. All products go through a traditional cycle: introduction, growth, maturity, saturation, decline and obsolescence. Sometimes it takes generations, sometimes it takes two or three months. Skateboards are a good example. They were introduced in early 1980 and grew to maturity by early autumn but the fad was all over by December. Lots of people made a lot of money on skateboards but most of them lost it again at the end of the cycle because they did not get out quickly enough. This all boils down to 'timing'.

It is often recommended that you keep an 'Ideas' file in which you and your employees can put down any feasible suggestions. Look at the prevailing market influences and consider whether or not you can afford to produce (in both monetary and physical terms) a new product. It may be too late once your competitors have introduced a new product to decide whether or not you should attempt to match it. Once you have borne all these considerations in mind, however, you will be wise to plan to move with the market force.

Let us consider the base of *Brut*, the range of men's toiletries, which was introduced many years ago as a very high-class product. It went through the inevitable cycle, and when it began to decline the company made it available through outlets like Boots, Woolworths and so on. In this way they gave new life to the product by widening the market. When sales began to drop off again, they introduced not just aftershave but also body lotion and talc, as well as all the other toiletries they already sold under a different brand-name. Once more they widened the product range and the market, and *Brut* took off again. Then when it began to decline once more they brought in Henry Cooper with a big advertising campaign to promote their products. The big companies can afford to do that – they have the resources – but as a smaller company you will not be able to take such an aggressive market line, and so you will have to be prepared to move with the market.

This is where market research helps. If you cannot afford to hire the services of a specialist firm, then compile a simple questionnaire and ask your sales force to circulate it. The information gained from it can then be analysed, and will help in making overall decisions about your product. Get to know your market-place and which products it can take; it is no use producing a walking, talking, tail-wagging toy if there are others like it on the market, or if potential buyers will not accept it.

What types of control are there?

1. THE ORGANISATION of the business itself is a control. The fact that there is an organisation with directors and divisional managers, with even the simplest of administrative/financial/sales/production functions belies this. The business is structured in a pyramid fashion. When applied to the company's organisation this means a formal workload/personnel ratio. When a company becomes either too top heavy (with too many senior managers or middle managers) or the opposite, where there are not enough senior/middle managers, then a reversal of the pyramid takes place. This is harmful for business and should be avoided at all costs.

2. SEGREGATION OF FUNCTIONS is a control much loved by accountants. The fact that, in a business, people will have to do different things to the same document is a form of control. In a typical situation one person in a department will, say, enter prices on an invoice, and that invoice will then be passed to somebody else who will check that price and perhaps extend it. If one person puts a wrong price on an invoice and benefits from it, the other person who checks it has to be brought into the scheme – there has to be collusion for the fraud to work. So in a wages department segregation of duty helps to prevent loss to the business.

3. PHYSICAL CONTROLS include the lock on the petty cash box, the fence round the factory, the list of who uses the company cars and how many miles they have done, who has the authority to order what, etc.

4. AUTHORISATION means that everything has to be approved by somebody. The most common example is that cheques can only be signed if they are authorised

by a senior manager in charge of that section. If there are two directors then a system should be arranged whereby two signatures are needed. Orders too, have to be signed by someone in authority to be valid.

5. ACCOUNTING CONTROLS include such things as someone going through invoices to check that they are added up correctly. Other examples are ensuring that ledgers are balanced, that bank statements are reconciled, that management accounts balance and that in annual accounts the balance sheet adds up. All outgoings and incomings should ideally be analysed and accounting controls established for prompt invoicing and credit control. The production of a profit/loss tells you the state of your cash flow and of the variables in addition to giving you a forewarning of any future problems (see Chapter 6).

6. PERSONNEL CONTROLS ensure that you employ people fit for the job, that they have had appropriate training, they know what to do and that they are reliable.

7. SUPERVISION of these members of staff is a form of control. If you have an invoicing section, there could be a need for a supervisor of that department, depending upon the size of your company and department and your turnover. If you have a shop, there will be one person there who is in charge of the other assistant(s). The staff then know that if they have a problem there is a supervisor to approach, and that they do not have to go right to the very top, which might put them off.

8. MANAGEMENT has the task of ensuring that the company's objectives are in line with their employee's job specifications, and that all jobs are carried out satisfactorily. They, along with the other employees and the owners, should have the company's best interests at heart, from making sure that the products

are selling at the right price and making the right profit, through receiving the cash and seeing that it does not go astray, to making sure that production is up to standard and looking after the welfare and status of the staff.

Cash management is a vital function in the overall management role, with the main aim being to generate more capital for the company, as well as to conserve the existing capital. There are a number of areas where this principle can be effectively applied, such as cost reduction, aggressive pricing, elimination of cash absorbers, liquidation of excess assets, and cautious borrowing. Credit control (see Chapter 6), prompt invoicing, good banking arrangements and payments to suppliers are all areas which need attention.

The continuous monitoring of a business is an important management function. Monitoring may be broadly defined as the preparation and review of regular accounting information. It should include preparation of budgets and costs flow forecasts, followed by the comparison of these projections with actual results on a regular basis.

The fact that your business is doing well does not mean that you can sit back; indeed, it can be said that you need to work even harder. Priorities need to be established concerning the day-to-day financial controls of the business and the regular reporting of results. Do not rely on the annual audit to determine the future of the company; by its nature, an audit deals in historical information and cannot normally be used to determine the strategy of the company.

The importance of regular financial information does not lie in its preparation; it is the intelligent review of the results and trends shown by that information which is essential to the successful running of the company. For example, the accounts may show that sales have fallen, but it is more important to understand why. There could be a simple answer, or the answer could rest with any one of a number of problems, from production problems to understaffing or defaulted deliveries. The information should be prepared on a

SAMPLE COMPANY LTD

MANAGEMENT ACCOUNTS FOR THE QUARTER ENDED:

Last year			This period				Cumulative to date			
Quarter	To date		Actual		Budget		Actual		Budget	
£000	£000		£000	%	£000	%	£000	%	£000	%
		SALES								
		Cost of Sales								
		GROSS PROFIT								
		Commission payable								
		Carriage and packing under (over) recovery								
		Bad debts provision								
		Rent and rates								
		Light, heat and power								
		Insurance								
		Repairs and renewals								
		Directors' remuneration								
		Other employment costs								
		Travelling and motor expenses								
		Printing, stationery and advertising								
		Telephone and postage								
		General expenses								
		Audit and other professional fees								
		Hire and leasing costs								
		Depreciation								
		Bank charges and interest								
		Other items (service charge receivable)								
		TOTAL OVERHEADS								
		NET PROFIT (LOSS) BEFORE TAXATION								

Reproduced by kind permission of Spicer and Pegler

Figure 5.1: Quarterly management account sheet

regular basis. It is a good idea to prepare these accounts monthly, near the middle or the end of the month.

Controls prevent you getting lost. If things go wrong you can find out why, and do something about it quickly. If your business is going into loss or stops making a profit, then your controls (management accounts, cash figures and cash flow forecast) will sound warning bells in time for you to take action. You will not be waiting until the end of the year or perhaps several months after that for your accountant to tell you that you have made a loss of £10,000 last year. Your controls will have warned you that this is happening and you can do something about it.

Controls also stop you breaking the law. If you pay people's wages without deducting tax, or pay the wrong amount of VAT or are not observing the Health and Safety at Work Act – then you are breaking the law. Controls in business prevent mistakes which, while they may be quite innocent, are nevertheless unlawful. Ignorance is no defence in the eyes of the law.

The essential thing for any business, large or small, is to have a strategy: to know where you are going and how you are going to get there. If you have the right controls then the organisation will follow naturally, and in turn you will be able to monitor your plans and see if they are on course and if not, why not. The following financial checklists will set you in the right direction.

Financial checklist

Cash control

Day-to-day financial management needs to be applied continuously, and in detail, to the ever-changing cycle of expenditure and revenue. In the course of this cycle, cash is converted into trading assets such as stock and work-in-progress, then into debtors and finally back into cash. The cash generated by this process should exceed that which is invested in it, and control is needed to maximise this process, to prevent leakage during the cycle, and to ensure that it moves as fast as possible. There follows a series of quotations to which you should already know the answers – if you don't then you should find them out.

Cash

Have you reviewed security arrangements and insurance?
How long is each element of the trading cycle?
What changes can be made to improve the cycle?
Are budgets expressed both as cash-flow and profit forecasts?
Can performance in cash flow be compared with expectations?
What is the regular difference between bank statement and cash book?
Are bankings sufficiently frequent?
Are bank accounts grouped for interest and bank charges purposes?
Ratio: cash and liquid assets/current liabilities

Stock and work-in-progress

Is stock kept securely and is it adequately insured?
Have you taken your accountant's advice on recording and valuation?
How much stock is surplus to expected requirements?
How many stockouts occur?
What is the cost of stockholding?
Are reorder quantities established and safety stocks reviewed?
How often can you determine stock levels?
How much production is for stock or for specific order?
Can stock lines be rationalised?
Are bulk orders cost-effective?
Do checking procedures prevent over-deliveries or damaged goods being accepted?
Can you identify and reduce slow-moving stock?
Can you time purchases to defer tax?
Ratio: stock/purchases
stock/sales
work-in-progress/production
seasonality and sales trends

Accounts receivable – debtors

What time lag occurs between sales and invoices?
Can payment on account or in advance be required?
Are invoices clear and correct?
Can direct debiting or bankers' orders be introduced?
What is the effect of discounts for prompt payments?
Is special clearing of large cheques worthwhile?
What about credit insurance?
What about debt factoring?
Are customers' credit ratings checked before accepting orders?
Have you considered a debt collection agency?
Do you ensure prompt and regular chasing of overdue accounts?
Ratio: debtors/sales (expressed in days)

Accounts payable – creditors

How many suppliers do you deal with?
Are there single sources suppliers of key materials?
Can payments be delayed?
Are buying costs known?
Are payment discounts worth taking?
Are all purchases properly authorised?
Could you pay twice for the same goods?
Price indices for main supplies.
Lead times for main suppliers.
Ratio: orders overdue/orders placed
creditors/purchases (days)
goods returns/purchases

Assets employed

Can you measure the use of assets in output, value, units?
Can you measure contribution from the output?
What is maximum capacity?
Are there any bottlenecks?
What are the fixed costs of the capacity?
What is the realisable value of assets employed?
Are assets properly insured?
Can you time investment or defer taxes?

Should you use discounted cash-flow techniques?
What are the advantages of buying, hiring or leasing?
Ratio: operating profit/operating assets
operating profit/sales
sales/operating assets
actual output/maximum output
unproductive time/total time

Capital structure

What proportion of funds are borrowed and on what terms?
Are loans due for early repayment?
Are corporate plans prepared?
Are cash-flow forecasts and plans available?
Is liquidity adequate?
Are there special tax considerations?
Have capital markets been explored?
What about the USM?
What about industrial co-operatives and management buyouts?
Ratio: profit before interest/total assets employed
borrowed money/equity
interest payable/borrowed money.

6 Bookkeeping and administrative systems

This chapter explains an essential aspect of your business: bookkeeping and administration. It describes a simple and easily kept system of administration and accounts that can be tailored to the needs of most small businesses.

A word of warning – do not try to run before you can walk. Start with simple systems and let them grow with you – your time is extremely valuable and you do not want to find yourself working at an over-complicated system far into the night. You may ask, Why have a system at all? Why keep the books? At the end of the day, the success or failure of your business is not measured primarily in the quality of your product, but in financial terms – in other words, profit. If, for instance, you forget a delivery date or miss invoicing, you will not get cash coming in. A permanent record of your business affairs is therefore required. The Inland Revenue will require its share of your profits, and they will demand – whether or not you have made a profit – financial statements at the end of each year which can be supported by documentary evidence. On these the Inspector of Taxes will base his demands. If the turnover of your business exceeds £23,600 per annum (at present rates), you will have to register with HM Customs and Excise and charge the relevant rate of VAT on your sales. You will be able to set off any VAT paid against VAT charged on incoming invoices. You will be required to keep adequate records and declare all VAT charged on a regular basis. The VAT inspector may come to check your records. To ensure that your business runs smoothly, you will need to set up systems for ordering and its control, a system for keeping your records in easily accessible files, and personnel records when you take on an employee, etc. All these aspects of your business require systems.

Book-keeping

For your own benefit it is necessary to monitor the well-being of your company, and you will wish to keep a close control of your cash flow and results. One of the major factors that contributes to the failure of many small businesses is a simple lack of financial control. Hard evidence of your trading record will always be required if you find it necessary to raise further capital or even to continue your bank overdraft.

So, what does bookkeeping entail and how do you go about it? Firstly, it involves a procedure for recording monetary transactions, both payments and receipts, and dealing with the associated paper work. This is done in such a way as to ensure that the information is readily accessible when you need to refer to it and is easy to understand. Secondly, the method of recording is designed to require a minimum of your time and effort. Finally, a level of control is provided to ensure that the information you are recording is correct.

At the end of the year you will probably need to employ an accountant to prepare the actual accounts and to submit them to the Inland Revenue. The more time he has to spend on your records the more he will charge you. Any work you can do during the year to write up your own books will save him time and you money.

Of course, each business is different, and has its own accounting requirements. The most important thing is to set up a bookkeeping system that can develop with your business. To start off you will require books to record:

— The analysed receipts and payments in your bank account;
— Your daily take, split, if necessary, into categories;
— Analysis of miscellaneous cash expenditure viz petty cash;
— Adequate VAT records;
— Adequate wages records;
— Means to file invoices, receipts, correspondence, etc.

Keep a separate book for your cash expenditure and cash incoming; the different types are discussed individually in the subsequent sections, and the books can be obtained from most large high street stationers. Take care, however, to choose the right one – compare the suggested rulings shown in this chapter with what is available and remember it is better to get one with too many columns rather than too few. Ensure that you keep an adequate filing system.

Finally, remember that your accountant, like your bank manager will prove an invaluable friend to your business. Do not hesitate to consult him and to act on his advice when you start. He will have a wealth of experience in dealing with new businesses and five minutes spent with you, even on the phone, can well save him hours at the end of the year as well as giving him, one hopes, a more successful client.

The cash book

The cash book is used to record and analyse all receipts and payments in your bank account. If it is written up regularly it will tell you instantly how much, or how little, money you have in the bank. This is something your bank statement will only tell you when you actually receive it, once a month.

The cash book is divided into two sections. Receipts are entered on the left-hand side and payments on the right. A suggested ruling is shown in Figure 6.1. You will note that there are only three columns of analysis for receipts; this is because your major income will usually be from sales, which can be sub-analysed through the sales day book. Think about the type of receipts you will expect to have in your business and if necessary choose an analysis book with more columns.

When you first start in business you will rarely require a purchase day book for sub-analysis of your expenditure; it is much easier to do this analysis in your cash book. Figure 6.1 shows a typical analysis, you must, however, tailor the headings to suit your own business; your accountant will be able to advise you on this. It cannot be over-emphasised that a detailed breakdown of your expenditure is of great importance to you and your business as well as for your accountant in producing your accounts at the end of the year.

You will note from the headings that sales receipts are itemised by individual invoice; this is by far the best method for small businesses. (When you come to file

Receipts

Date	Detail	ref.	Bank	Sales	Sundry	(description)	
1989	brought forward		823.26	523.26	300.00		
Feb 11	B Jones	101		153.00			
	T. Andrews	103		127.36			
	M. Stokes	106	636.36	356.00			
12	A. Baker	107		54.00			
	T. Smith		116.00		62.00	Sale of cabinet	
14	K Brown		743.87	743.87			
28	B. White	137		129.00			
	T. Green	139	1157.00	1028.00			
			3476.49	3114.49	362.00		
March 1	Balance b/d		103.64		103.64		

Payments

Date	Detail	cheque no.
1989	brought forward	
Feb 15	Sperean Ltd	363012
	Brit. Telecom	" [illegible]
16	Alf's Garage	" [illegible]
	Bronkhort's	" [illegible]
	Brown's	" [illegible]
	Printers Ltd	" [illegible]
17	Ins. Brokers Ltd	" [illegible]
	Cash	" [illegible]
28	A. White	3[illegible]
	Inland Revenue	3[illegible]
	Balance c/d	

Figure 6.1: Cash book

Bank	VAT	Materials	Elec/Gas	Stat./Post	Telephone	Travel Exp.	Motor Exp.	Repair	Rent/Rates Ins.	Wages/PAYE	Petty Cash	Sundries (description)	
962.37	147.26	406.97	14.03	82.73		12.03	38.92		79.83		107.14	73.46	
62.38	8.14	54.24											
164.76	14.72				150.04								
83.96	10.95						73.01						
172.50	22.50											150.00	Accountancy
083.96	141.38	942.58											
54.73	7.14			47.59									
117.15									117.15				
114.08											114.08		
450.82										450.82			
106.14										106.14			
103.64												103.64	
3476.49	352.09	1403.79	14.03	130.32	150.04	12.03	111.93		196.98	556.96	221.22	327.10	

these invoices away number them in sequence, noting the number in your ledger book. This will make for a quick and easy referral.)

Receipts

As you receive money, either by cheque or in cash, you will want to pay it into your bank account. This you will do by entering each item's details into your paying-in book and presenting it and the cheque, or cash, at the bank. Enter the details from the paying-in book into the receipts side of the cash book, recording sales in the sales column, sundry receipts in the sundries column, etc., making sure that all items add across to the total amount entered in the bank column. This should be the amount shown subsequently on your bank statement. If items are credited directly to your bank account you will also have to enter these in your cash book.

Payments

You will draw cheques on your bank account and in the same way you will enter these on the payments side, making sure that the total of the individual cheques and the relevant details are clearly entered. The analysis of the expenditure is then entered into the relevant column. If you are registered for VAT you will have to enter the VAT amount in the VAT column leaving only the net amount to be entered in the analysis column. Similarly, items appearing directly in your bank statements such as standing order payments, bank charges, etc., will also have to be entered in your cash book.

Keep a running total of the two bank columns, the difference between the two will give you your bank balance. At the end of each month, total up all the columns and enter the totals. All the subsidiary columns should add back to the two bank columns. If they do not, then check your additions and the analysis of your items – five minutes spent now will be amply rewarded in the future. When both sides agree enter the balance to equal up to receipts and payments.

The bank reconciliation

When you receive your bank statement covering your transactions up to the end of the month, tick off the items, both receipts and payments, in your cash book. In so doing you will find the following items, apart from those which appear in both the statement and your cash book.

(a) Receipts and payments not entered in your cash book. Enter these (see on page 92).
(b) Items in your cash book but not in the statements. If these are receipts, check to see whether they have been credited by the bank in the first few days of the next month and list these. If they are cheques they are probably 'outstanding', meaning that it may be some time before the payee of the cheque pays it into his own bank and it is presented, through the clearing bank, to your own bank. Again, list these.

You can then prepare a reconciliation as shown below.

Bank reconciliation as at 28 February 19——

Balance from bank statement (overdrawn)		(455.95)
Add receipts credit 2 March 19——		1,157.00
		701.05
Less outstanding cheques	£450.82	
	£106.14	
	£40.45	£597.41
Balance as per cash book		£103.64

If it reconciles, pat yourself on the back. You have probably written your cash book up correctly. If it does not then you will have to look for the difference. Again, do not begrudge the time.

The evidence

As you enter up your cash book, make sure you have some evidence for every entry. On the receipts side it will be your daily takings record, your sales day book (see Figure 6.3) or a note about a sundry receipt. On the payment side it will be the electricity bill, the purchase invoice, the garage bill, etc. Cross reference all these to your cash book and file them in date and number order.

The result

The monthly totals for each column will show your expenditure for the month in each category. The monthly figures will make up the annual figures that will appear in your accounts.

Sales day book

If your business is in retail, or you only take cash, or if you issue your invoices and collect payment at the same time, it would be simple for you to record your sales directly in the cash book. In this case, you will need a book with a few more columns on the receipts side, according to the detail you need, and of course, a column for VAT analysis if you are registered. You will not need to keep a separate sales book.

If you do issue invoices in advance (see Figure 6.2) of receiving payment, then your cash receipts will not reflect your sales on a daily basis; you therefore need to keep a separate record of the sales invoices that you issue. Use a sales day book for this purpose.

If you are registered for VAT (and even if you are not) you should keep a record of each invoice you issue. It helps to have printed invoices in sets, so that for instance, the top white copy goes to your customer, the second copy (green) is for your accounting copy filed in numerical order, and the third copy (blue) goes in the individual customer file. The VAT regulation lays down what information should be shown on an invoice and an example is shown in Figure 6.2.

As you issue your invoice, enter it in your sales day book as shown in Figure 6.3. Again, you will note the individual details shown for each invoice. You have the choice, with two or more columns to split your sales between types. Note that the VAT is shown separately

SUPPLIERS
54 High Street
Newtown NA2 3QZ
Telephone: 0803 96481

SALES INVOICE NO

INVOICE ADDRESS	DELIVERY ADDRESS (if different)

Your Order No	Contract No	Date and Tax Point

Description	Quantity	Price	Tax Exclusive Value	VAT Rate	VAT Payable
			£	%	£
		Tax Exclusive Value	£	%	£
		Plus VAT	£		
		Invoice Value	£		

TERMS OF PAYMENT

VAT No 300 3000 03

Figure 6.2: Sales invoice

Sales Day-Book

Date	Detail	Inv. No	Amount ①	Amount ②	VAT	Invoice total	Amount paid	Discount	Data paid
1986									
Feb 1	F. Ingram	112	47.00		7.05	54.05	52.70	1.35	3.2.85
	B. Jones	113	738.00		110.70	848.70	827.48	21.22	6.2.85
	I. Smith	114		110.00	16.50	126.50	123.34	3.16	8.2.85
	T. Andrews	115	110.75		16.61	127.36	127.36	–	11.2.85
2	J. Press	116		382.00	57.30	439.30	428.32	10.98	5.2.85
28	Blocks	157	173.62		26.04	199.66			
	Polygraphic			28.42	4.26	32.68			
			1069.37	520.42	238.46	1828.25	1559.20	36.71	

Figure 6.3: Sales day book

Receipts			Payments											
Date	Detail	Cash	Date	Detail	Voucher No.	TOTAL	VAT	Post.	Stat.	Travel	Motor expenses	Clean	Sundries	
1986			1986											
Feb 1	Balance B/f	270.00	Feb 1	Postage	41	18.00		18.00						
			2	Cleaners	42	8.40						8.40		
				Mr. White	43	115.71	8.38		16.03	90.31			1.00	Telephone
			3	Petrol for van	44	11.50	1.50				10.00			
17	Cash book	107.14	4	Grocers Ltd	45	63							63	Coffee
			10	Mr. Smith	46	171.86	22.43		149.43					
26	Cash book	114.08												
				Total		326.10	32.31	18.00	165.46	90.30	10.00	8.40	1.63	
			Feb 28	Balance		165.12								
		491.22				491.22								
March 1	Balance	165.12												

Figure 6.4: Petty cash book

and that only the *net* amount is analysed. Make sure you file the copy of the invoice in the same order.

All being well, your customers will pay your invoices, and when they do, enter the amount and date in the columns provided. If you allow them a discount for prompt payment, then enter the discount given in the appropriate column so that the amount received plus the discount clears the invoice amount. If your customer settles more than one invoice at a time, cross-reference the receipt to the respective invoices. If you issue credit notes make sure these are entered, placing the details in brackets to show that they should be deducted, in the sales day book.

The receipts entered will form the amounts that are paid into your bank and will be shown in the cash book.

At any time the invoices with no 'paid' entry against them will be those that are unpaid. You will then be in a position to remind the client via a letter, phone call or statement. Similarly, after the end of the year, your accountant will be able to pick out those unpaid by the year end by checking the dates of subsequent payment.

Each month, total up the columns and enter the totals, checking that subsidiary columns including VAT balance by adding across to the total. This total will be your monthly sales, including VAT, whilst your cash book figure will be the cash received from your customers. Any difference will be cash received during the month from invoices issued in the previous month or conversely, invoices issued but still unpaid.

Petty cash book

The petty cash book is used to record small items of expenditure which you pay for in cash. Figure 6.4 illustrates a typical lay-out for a petty cash book although, again, you must tailor the headings of analysis to suit your business.

Receipts of cash from the bank are shown on the left-hand side and expenditure on the right-hand side. The easiest method of dealing with petty cash is to draw an initial 'float' of cash for you to hold, preferably in the petty cash box. When any expenditure is made, a petty cash numbered voucher is marked and usually at the end of every week the vouchers are entered in numerical order in the petty cash book. The book is totalled regularly and you then draw a cheque for the total spent in order to 'top up' your float to the original level. Vouchers should always be kept for your accountant at the end of the year and are probably easiest kept in marked envelopes.

The petty cash book should be reconciled monthly so that the balance in the book – the difference between the two sides – should equal the money in the box. If it does not you have probably forgotten to enter some item of expenditure. Note that there is a VAT column and that the analysis is net of VAT.

At the end of each month the subsidiary columns are totalled and agreed by adding across to the total column. As with the cash book, the balance is carried forward to the next month.

Wages book

You will have to keep a wages book and employee records as soon as you start employing others to help you run your business. It is necessary to follow the rules of the Inspector of Taxes and your accountant will assist you in this. It is advisable to arrange all this before you take on any employees so that you will be able to start paying them correctly as soon as they start work.

The Inspector of Taxes will send you the relevant booklets explaining how Income Tax and National Insurance contributions are deducted from the wages you pay to your staff and remitted to the Collector of Taxes. The Inspector will also send you stationery on which to record the individual employees' deduction.

In addition to this, you will need a wages book to summarise weekly or monthly payments made. There are several available on the market and Figure 6.5

Month Ending FEB 86 Week No. ______

NAME	National Insurance No	Contribution Table Letter	Gross Amount Due	EMPLOYER'S DEDUCTIONS				Net Amount Due	EMPLOYER'S CONTRIBUTIONS	
				Tax	Class 1				Class 1	
A. White (Code 220L)	7/K 0/1 2/1 1/9 B	A	636.07	135.82	57.42			443.05	66.67	

Figure 6.5: Wages book

illustrates a typical lay-out. It is also necessary to keep personal records of each of your employees, giving:

Full name
Address
Date of birth
National Insurance number
Date of starting work with you
Salary
Position held
Date of leaving if relevant

You will need to give your employees payslips which detail how their wages are made up. You will also need to keep records of your employees' absences due to illness and you are required to compute and pay to them sickness pay, which is then reclaimed from your payment to the Collector of Taxes. This is called Statutory Sick Pay and the Inspector of Taxes will furnish you with all relevant forms and documents regarding this. (Chapter 9 discusses the details of recruitment and employment law.)

Irrespective of whether you pay your staff weekly or monthly, you will need to draw a cheque or cash to pay them. This will be entered in the cash book or petty cash book as will the cheque drawn to remit to the Inland Revenue, for the PAYE and National Insurance deductions. Note that the employer also contributes to National Insurance.

Summarise your wages book and check that the figures agree with the wages column of your cash book. The figure that will appear in your accounts will be the gross cost of the wages, that is, the net amount paid to employees plus the PAYE and National Insurance deducted, plus the employer's contribution. The wages book should give you the breakdown of this figure.

Individual entries should agree with the tax deduction cards supplied by the Inland Revenue. Wages envelopes with a printed summary on the outside are readily available. If you have more than a few employees it is probably a good idea to look at one of the proprietary systems which allows you to deal with the pay slips, wages book and deduction card all at the same time.

Remember that if your business is a limited company and you are a director, even if you are the sole director or jointly with your wife, then any money taken from the firm will be your wages and should be taxed through the PAYE system. The Inland Revenue is now quite strict about this and will penalise directors for drawing untaxed lump sum amounts.

If you are a sole trader or partnership then your tax is assessed on your real results and the amounts you take are your drawings. These do not have to be taxed at the time, but remember that you are still liable to pay National Insurance and will have to pay, depending on your results, tax on your profits sometime in the future.

VAT

For most small businesses, the VAT is relatively easy to complete, always given that your books are kept up to date and totalled on a regular basis. If you have followed the advice of the earlier parts of this chapter then you will have already recorded all the details necessary for completing the VAT return.

It is advisable to keep a separate book for your VAT workings. Figure 6.6 gives an example of this. The information for items 1 to 8 in the official VAT return are in the VAT column of the book and the information required in items 9 and 10 is given in the 'totals excluding VAT' columns. Do be especially careful not to claim in the input column any VAT paid over to HM Customs and Excise. This is a very common mistake; unfortunately they do not take kindly to you boosting your income by claiming back the VAT already paid over. VAT is discussed in detail in the following chapter.

Credit control

This area is very important to the continued success of your business. It relies on information found in the sales book and cash book previously covered.

What are your terms of credit? And how long do your

clients take to pay? Are you currently overdrawn at the bank and still owed outstanding monies?

It is a fallacy to believe that applied credit control will upset your customers. What is the point of selling your product if you are not going to get paid? If done in a proper and efficient way, credit control is not only effective but will not offend your clients. They will respect you for it as they in turn have to do the very same thing.

Do not be heavy handed. Your first action should be a statement of account sent out between 14 days and 21 days after the invoice (or with an existing credit chasing system) or at the end of every month. After a reasonable period of time, a pleasant telephone call to your customer's 'bought ledger' department should gain some response. Again allow a few weeks to elapse and then if nothing happens send a polite letter as a reminder that the account is now overdue by 'XX' days and that you would appreciate prompt settlement of the outstanding amount. A rapport often builds up between yourself and the 'bought ledger' and if this is kept on a pleasant business footing then you can succeed in calling in outstanding money where a hard-handed approach will often fail to win prompt action. You should not, unless it is absolutely necessary, resort to solicitors' letters. Should recovery, after completing the credit-chasing procedure, become difficult you can try to reclaim the debt by issuing a summons in the small claims section of the County Court.

After some time a pattern will emerge showing you the clients who pay promptly and those who take longer to settle their account. Large firms will often take 60 days to 90 days to settle, sometimes longer than that, so do ensure that this is taken into account, or if not acceptable, that the matter has already been discussed with your client and credit terms agreed.

If a client is consistently overdue in paying your invoices, to the extent of using between 60 and 90 days over and above the credit term agreed, then you should consider whether or not to withdraw credit terms or to

Page 4

VAT return period 1.2.86 – 30.4.86

			Total (excluding VAT)	VAT
Output (sales)				
Sales daybook	February	①	1069.37	160.40
		②	520.42	78.06
	March	①	2037	305.55
		②	1875	281.25
	April	①	1248	187.20
		②	1029	154.35
			7778.79	1166.81
Inputs (purchases & expenses) (exclude exempt)				
	February		3124.70	352.09
	March		2110	206.48
	April		2896	388.27
Petty Cash	February		293.79	32.31
	March		382	26.14
	April		403	28.72
			9209.49	1034.01
Balance payable/(receivable)				132.80
				paid 3/6/86

Figure 6.6: VAT return sheet

cease trading with them. This decision, of course, rests entirely with you and should not be taken lightly. If either eventuality occurs, do make it clear to your client the reason why the step has had to be taken.

If you allow a discount for prompt payment do ensure that, should the client not pay within the time, the discount is not deducted from the paid invoiced amount.

Administrative systems

This section is based on administrative principles vital to the success of an existing or proposed small business. It also assumes that you know in detail the product or service of your business.

Paperwork and legislative controls hold little attraction for many people – indeed, most would tell you that they hate paperwork – but they are essential to the success of a business. These controls do not have to be either time-consuming or sophisticated.

Earlier in the book you will have read about how to obtain additional finance, whether or not it is best to operate in a partnership or as a sole trader, and rules on sales and marketing. Basically, in operating your business you will have three main factors to consider:

— The knowledge of your product/service;
— Money;
— People.

Each of these areas require records and administrative procedures of one sort or another to comply with statutory or just sound business requirements.

Simple systems

How well do you know your product or service? Have you put your message across to your target market? If you have told people about your product, have you got a record of whom you have told?

To get a system started, compile a contact list of all those who you believe would benefit from buying from you. This list could contain people or companies who you already know. By using a simple card index system you will have a growing record of adresses for communications, plus details of previous sales and payments and any other relevant information about each target company or the persons running it (see Figure 6.7). Start off by recording details of local firms and expand it geographically as time goes by. This is all common sense but there are many businesses who do not have even such a simple record – when asked why not, they say 'we are too busy'!

When selling your product or service, the next thing to do is to produce a printed information sheet. The size and style is entirely up to you. However, ensure that the information it contains is accurate. Once you have these leaflets, one can be given out to each person who expresses an interest in your product or service. Remember to make a note of the name, address and telephone number of each contact, recording all these details (and the price quoted them) on your record cards.

NAME	TELEPHONE NO.
ADDRESS	TELEX NO.
	FAX NO.
	CONTACT NAME
	PRICE QUOTED

INITIAL APPROACH VIA
RESULT

DETAILS OF SALE

DATE	ORDER NO.	QUANTITY	PRODUCT	DELIVERY DATE	INVOICE NO.

Figure 6.7: Sales contact card

The next area to examine when implementing systems is the financial one. If you go to a bank for additional funds the first thing you will be asked is, 'How soon can you pay it back?' and/or 'Can you let me have a cash flow statement?' This cash flow statement is a vital part of your administrative records. It must project for at least a year ahead, preferably three years, and it must show what bills you expect to receive month by month for rent, rates, light and heating purchases, wages, even VAT. You then must estimate the volume of your sales over the same period – remember to be realistic when working on future projections. Then and only then can you estimate what your cash balance or overdraft figure is likely to be at the end of each month. Naturally, any hire purchase, leasing or loan repayments must be similarly noted.

Accounts records should be kept and an explanation of what books to keep and how to keep them has already been described. You must, however, remember to set aside time to keep these accounts up to date and accurate otherwise the entire accounts system will grind to a halt. Another area often forgotten is your existing stock level. This stock represents money tied up and not available for use.

Whether it is for your own use or for resale, what is the level of your stock? Stock records, kept up to date, can tell you what the present level of stock is, with the added bonus that they can also tell you the length of time the stock has been held, and the quantities, and you can then do something about it where necessary. If you review stock records regularly, you can see at a glance what is moving and what is not, and this can be a great help in controlling the capital outlay necessary when keeping stock up to the right level. Again you need a simple card index showing commodity, pack, supplier, minimum and maximum stock, incomings and outgoings, and balance with a value column.

An even simpler way of keeping a check on supplies used in your business is the method operated by an efficient housewife in her food cupboard – have two of everything and when you use one replace it! By using one system you can effect a simple order control.

Another area of administration to look at is personnel. All details relating to your employees must be assigned a file – one file for each individual. All appropriate records must be kept in this file, such as job application forms, references, your copy of the contract of employment, letter of appointment, etc. These files must be kept private and confidential and noted as such. Notes from discussions should also be filed away and any letters of complaint too. Wages cards (and your account files and books) can also be kept in the private and confidential filing drawer as this will save on space initially.

Keep copies to hand of the different leaflets given out by the Department of Employment and the Department of Social Security. A list of useful leaflets is given in Chapter 9.

The key to good administration is to keep it simple, creating a file only if you really need it. A correspondence filing system is the most basic and the easiest to start; all you need to do is put one client's correspondence in one file, that of another client in the next file, and so on. You then build up these files and put them away alphabetically. Your business administration files should be divided into six parts – office, personnel, legal, accounting, equipment (purchases) and sales (customers). Keep the files separate at all times, preferably in a safe, fireproof location. Do consider keeping duplicate records. Should any unforeseen accident occur, such as a fire, it would take some time to compile replacement documentation. Consider purchasing a safe in which to place your valuables. Your office insurance could be reduced should you acquire a safe.

A first-aid kit will have to be purchased and a first-aid system set up. It is extremely important that your office and/or factory complies with the Health and Safety at Work Act. The Department of Employment will send you all the necessary details; you may already have had a visit from your local factory inspector to ensure that you are complying with the Act. A book will need to be kept to record any accidents.

What about office equipment – should you buy or lease it? If you are a new company starting up you could find leasing difficult to obtain. On the other hand, if you purchase, you are allowed to write off part of the value of the machine each year. As there are so many different machines, at varying prices, it is often best to look at the situation carefully in the light of your own requirements and business. If you are thinking about buying a micro-computer, do shop around and decide what sort of work you want the machine to do. However, unless you have a manual system up and working it is pointless trying to match a computer program in order to take over the existing workload. You must know what you need and want from a system before you buy it. Many companies have run into serious administrative difficulties (and financial ones too) over the purchase of a micro-computer. Telegraph Publications has produced a comprehensive book on micro-computers entitled *How to Choose and Use Business Microcomputers and Software* which will be most helpful.

Part of successful administration is making sure that your business is covered by insurance. Obtain quotations and compare the price and content of different policies as they vary, and do read the small print. You are required by law to have a policy called 'Employer's Liability' and the policy must be displayed in a prominent position. Your machinery, premises, vehicle, etc. will all need to be covered by insurance.

Administration is just as important an ingredient in the success of a business as the rest of the business disciplines. To run a business you have to amalgamate the various skills involved, and you will find that at any one time one particular skill will be needed more than the others. But remember that clear and simple administrative systems will ensure that you will not run foul either of the law, the various government departments or your customers.

The 'Select Bibliography' on page 206 is a useful reference should you wish to locate a book that goes into more detail on a specific business or financial topic.

7 National Insurance, corporation tax and VAT

'No man in this country is under the smallest obligation, moral or otherwise, so to arrange his legal relations to his business or to his property as to enable the Inland Revenue to put the largest possible shovel into his stores.'

This was Lord President Clyde's view, adding that the taxpayer is 'entitled to be astute to prevent, so far as he honestly can, the depletion of his means by the Revenue'.

When you start your business, you have to decide the form it is going to take: sole trader, partnership, unlimited liability or limited liability company. The tax position can decide which form you start off with, although no good tax adviser will ignore the commercial requirements. But just a slight adjustment here and there can make a material difference to the amount of tax that you pay – not only to the amount but also to when it is paid. At the end of this chapter you will find an invaluable summary of the key points which you need to know about tax and your business. (While every effort has been made to ensure that the figures given in this chapter are correct, please refer to the latest DSS and Inland Revenue leaflets for the most up-to-date figures.)

National Insurance

Although we talk of National Insurance (NI) as 'contributions', it is, of course, just another form of taxation. NI is easy for the government to levy as it is an efficient system of collecting tax; it does not cause too much aggravation or need many staff to administer it.

National Insurance is often the forgotten element in tax planning. The amount involved these days can be quite considerable and it can tip the balance when you are trying to decide whether or not to set up as a sole trader, partnership, or whether to start off straight away as a limited liability company. One practical point to remember when employing additional staff is that the employer, in addition to deducting NI from that person, also has to pay to the government its own NI contribution. The rates of NI contributions effective from 6 April 1989 are as follows.

Table 7.1. Contracted in on all earnings. NI Class 1 contributions to 5 October 1989

On all earnings	**Employees** %	**Employers** %
Up to £42.99 per week	Nil	Nil
Between £43 and £74.99 per week	5	5
Between £75 and £114.99 per week	7	7
Between £115 and £164.99 per week	9	9
Between £165 and £325 per week	9	10.45
On excess over £325	max £29.25	10.45

Contracted in on all earnings. NI Class 1 contributions from 6 October 1989 to 5 April 1990

Employers: No charge	
Employees:	
below £43	Nil
between £1 and £43 of earned income	2
£43 to £325	9
maximum payable	£26.24

You will see that, up to £325 per week, these rates apply to all earnings, and this can have an adverse effect where an employee is paid on or just above the level where the rates change. If you were to pay someone £45 per week (up to 5 October 1989) then both you and that person would be liable to Class 1 on the whole of that person's earnings. So that extra £2 per week can lead to a reduction in take-home pay for your employee and an increase in overheads for you. At the other end of the scale, although an employee does not have to pay contributions on any earnings above £235 per week, (£16,900 a year), his employer is liable for NI at 10.45 per cent on all the employee's earnings without limit. (The upper limit that previously applied to employer's contributions was abolished on 6 October 1985.) For

Table 7.2. Contracted out; on all earnings, NI Class 1 contributions from 6 April 1989 to 5 October 1989

	Employees %	**Employers** %
Up to £42.99 per week	Nil	Nil
Up to £74.99 per week;		
on first £43	5	5
on balance	3	1.20
Up to £114.99		
on first £43	7	7
on balance	5	3.20
Up to £164.99		
on first £43	9	9
on balance	7	5.20
Up to £324.99		
on first £43	9	10.45
on balance	7	6.65
On excess over £325	max £23.61	£23.24 plus 6.65% on excess

Contracted out NI Class 1 contributions after 6 October 1989

Employer: As above but on the Slice of Earnings £43 to £325 per week the rates are reduced by 3.8 per cent for employers.

Employee: As above but on the Slice of Earnings £43 to £325 per week the rates are reduced by 2 per cent for employees.

this reason the Chancellor introduced in his 1989 Budget a flat rate charge of 2 per cent National Insurance contributions on the first £43 of earnings. The stepped rates of NI, i.e. 5 per cent and 7 per cent, were abolished. Earnings from £43 to £325 attract a second rate of 9 per cent. Overall this results in a reduction of NI for the top wage earners of £3.01 per week. If you or your employees are contracted out of the state pension schemes then you pay at reduced rates on the amount of salary over the lower earnings limit. Your maximum NI for any one year is worked out on the basis of contributions on 53 weeks at the upper limit.

If, however, you have a contracted out workforce, Table 7.2 shows you the 1989/90 rates.

NI for the self-employed

You are classed as self-employed if you are working entirely on your own account as a sole trader, or if you are a member of a partnership and not operating through a limited liability company; then you are liable to two NI classes: Classes 2 and 4. Class 2 is a flat-rate contribution of £4.25 per week. You simply buy a stamp at the Post Office each week or pay by direct debit. There are age limits and also exemptions for low earners.

The Class 4 contribution in 1989/90 amounts to a payment, in addition to the flat-rate contribution, of 6.3 per cent on your profits or gains between £5,050 and £16,900. You only pay on the amount in between those two figures. If you do not earn over £5,050 then you do not pay the initial 6.3 per cent. There is no great benefit to the self-employed from paying the Class 4 contributions although, as of 6 April 1986, 50 per cent of Class 4 contributions can obtain income tax relief. The benefits available to the self-employed through their Class 2 and 4 contributions are a great deal less than those to which employees and directors are entitled through their Class 1 contributions (see Table 7.3).

Table 7.3. Classes 2 and 4 self-employed 1988/89

Class 2 fixed per week	
no liability if earning below £2,350	£4.25
Class 4 earnings related	
on profits between £5,050 and £16,900 a year (see *Note*)	6.3%

Note. Half these contributions are allowable for income tax purposes.

NI for the unemployed

Class 3 a voluntary contribution by the unemployed (the official term is 'non-employed'). If you are in the happy state of being able to live entirely off your investments but would like to ensure some sort of NI benefits, then for 1989/90 you can make a voluntary payment of £4.15 per week.

NI: an outline

The employed

Class 1 contributions are in general payable by employees over the age of 16. Contributions are normally paid by the employee and the employer. However, if the employee has reached pensionable age (65 for men, and 60 for women) only the employer has to pay the contributions. Employers are required to deduct contributions from the employee's pay and to pay over the total to the Inland Revenue along with income tax deducted under the PAYE scheme.

— Rates of contribution are expressed as a percentage of earnings where these are at present between the 'earnings limits', which are in turn expressed in weekly, monthly or yearly terms to be used according to the normal pay intervals of the employee. Earnings limits and the new NI Class 1 rates are as shown on page 114.

— No contributions are payable if earnings are below the lower earnings limit subject to rules for persons with more than one employment.

— Where earnings fall in a particular bracket, contributions are payable at the rates indicated for that bracket on the full amount of the employee's earnings.

Where the employer has an occupational pension scheme which satisfies certain requirements, he can 'contract out' of the state scheme. The full rates apply to the part of the earnings up to the lower earnings limit but there is a reduced rate for the part of the earnings in excess of that figure.

— Earnings for contribution purposes are gross earnings before PAYE or pension fund deductions, but do not include redundancy payments, payments in lieu of notice, termination payments, pensions, benefits in kind, meal vouchers, expenses, or tips not paid by the employer.
— Primary contributions due from an employee with more than one employment in one year are limited to a maximum of the full rate applied to 53 weeks times the weekly upper earnings limit. There is normally no limit on the employer's contributions.
— There are special rules for persons entering or leaving the country. These may be modified if the movement is between EEC countries or between Great Britain and a country with whom it has a reciprocal agreement.

The self-employed

— Self-employed persons over 16 and under 65 (men) or 60 (women) can be liable to pay flat-rate Class 2 contributions and earnings-related Class 4 contributions. There are exemptions from Class 2 contributions, the most important being if earnings (as shown by the accounts) are expected to be below £2,350 for 1989/90.
— The rate of the Class 2 contribution is £4.25 per week. Contributions may be paid by purchasing stamps or by direct debit through a bank account or Giro.
— Earnings-related Class 4 contributions for any year are based on the profit assessable under Schedule D Class I or II for that year, after taking account of

capital allowances, balancing charges, loss relief, and annual payments incurred for trading purposes. For 1989/90 the rate of contribution is 6.3 per cent on assessable profits between £5,050 and £16,900 per annum. The businessman can obtain 50 per cent relief for income tax purposes on his graduated Class 4 contributions.

— Class 4 contributions are collected along with income tax on the Schedule D Class I or II assessment.

— Where a person is both employed and self-employed, his total maximum contribution under NI Classes 1, 2 and 4 is equal to 53 weekly Class 1 contributions on the upper earnings limit at the standard rate.

The unemployed

— Class 3 contributions are entirely voluntary and are payable by those who wish to secure a measure of entitlement to benefits and whose contribution record is not otherwise good enough. Class 3 contributions can only be paid by a person who has not paid, in Class 1 or 2, contributions equal to 52 Class 1 contributions at the standard rate on the lower weekly earnings limit.

— The rate is £4.15 per week. Contributions are paid by stamping a card or direct through a bank account or Giro.

Business tax

For the individual

If you go into business as an individual or in partnership, then your profits will be assessed to income tax. If you choose to operate through a UK limited liability company you will be liable to pay corporation tax on the chargeable profits of that company.

If you are a sole trader or partnership setting up business, you are entitled to count as part of your trading expenses any revenue expenditure incurred by you in connection with the business for up to five years before you actually started trading. For example, you may own a workshop for some three to six months before starting any work in it. But you are going to be paying rent, and you may have other outgoings such as gas and electricity. You can offset those against the income that you eventually generate when you do start trading. Those expenses, plus for example, capital allowances, can normally be used to reduce your profit or generate an income tax loss if you are setting up on your own. If you make an income tax loss then there are all sorts of things that you can do with the loss: you can carry it forward against the future income from your trade; if you have other income in the same year in which you make the loss, then you can set that loss off immediately against the other income; or you can save it up and if you are then still trading set it off against your income in the following year.

Furthermore, if you make an income tax loss in the first four years of trading, it can be carried back and set off against your other income in the three years prior to the loss. Remember, if you have a capital loss on a chargeable asset, you can set that off against capital gains in the same period or you can carry that capital loss forward. But you *cannot* set a capital loss against income – that is a basic rule of revenue law.

If you are an established self-employed person, whether working as a sole trader or as a partner, you pay tax on what is known as the preceding year basis. That is, you pay tax on the profits of the accounts which ended in the preceding tax year, so for the year 1988/89 your income tax is based on the profits of the business year ending 1987/88. There can be a considerable cash-flow benefit in this. If you pitch your accounting date at 30 April for income tax, your accounts to 30 April 1988 will form the basis of assessment for 1989/90 – you will pay half your tax on 1 January 1990 and half on 1 July 1990 so there will be a substantial period where you have the use of the money required eventually to pay your tax bills.

For your company

For companies it is a lot simpler. They just pay tax on a current year basis, on whatever they earn in the particular accounting period. Companies pay corporation tax on both income and capital gains. Capital gains tax, a tax rate of 30 per cent as from the 1988 Budget will no longer apply. Instead, the tax rate applicable will be linked to the level of income for the relevant year. This will apply to companies and individuals alike.

You calculate your trading income on normal accounting principles. In other words, not on a cash basis but on an invoicing basis, so you count the income when you become entitled to it rather than when you actually receive the cash. Similarly with expenditure, you bring in the liability when it arises, not when you pay out the money. That is the only type of income dealt with on that basis. Most other income is dealt with on a receipts basis.

For most companies the date of payment for corporation tax will generally be nine months after the end of the accounting period. (There are special rules that apply to companies that were in business before 1965, which is the date when corporation tax was introduced.) If the companies receive income from which income tax has been deducted they are given credit for that, and it is set off against the corporation tax due. If they have no profits liable for CT, they get the income tax back.

Table 7.4. Corporation tax

	Accounting period ended 31 March			
	1990	**1989**	**1988**	**1987**
Full rate	35%	35%	35%	35%
Small companies rate	25%	25%	27%	29%
Charged up to	£150,000	£100,000	£100,000	£100,000
Marginal relief up to	£750,000	£500,000	£500,000	£500,000
Marginal rate	37.5%	37.5%	37%	36.5%
Small companies fraction	1/40	1/40	1/50	3/200
Advanced CT	25/75ths	25/75ths	27/73rds	29/71sts

What are your allowances?

Once you have calculated your total profits, there are certain things you can deduct. The main element is non-bank interest paid for business purposes. If you pay interest to someone other than a bank, it is allowed not against your trading income but against your total profits. So, if you knock off the non-banking interest, you arrive at the profit chargeable for CT.

Marginal small companies' relief

Below £150,000 profits you pay 25 per cent and over £750,000 you pay 35 per cent in 1989/90. In between these two amounts is the 'marginal small companies' relief'. This is an effective tax rate of 37.5 per cent for year ending 31 March 1990. For a family company, making reasonable profits slightly over £150,000, it may be worth paying out extra cash to, say, directors' bonuses. In addition, it is worth taking on a little more plant and equipment and paying in a little more to the company's pension scheme in order to stay out of this £150,000 plus band, which results in you paying CT at 37.5 per cent on the difference between £150,000 and £750,000.

The limits of £750,000 and £150,000 are reduced if you have more than one company under your control, or more than one company in a group of companies. It would be very nice, of course, if you were making £400,000 just to set up four companies, with £100,000 profits at 25 per cent tax on each. However, it does not work that way.

What are dividends?

In small companies the shareholders and directors are usually the same. If you have any surplus profits they can be allocated as director's bonuses, in which case they will count as earned income. If, however, you take out the cash as a dividend, you will not get a deduction from the profits on the amounts that you pay out, which you do with the director's bonus.

If a company does pay a dividend, it hands over the

cash to the shareholders but it also pays advance corporation tax at 25/75ths (ending 31 March 1990) of the dividend. This figure is linked to the basic rate of income tax. It is called advance corporation tax because the company can set it off against its own corporation tax liability for the period in which it pays the dividend. The shareholder will get the cash dividend and a slip of paper with 'tax credit' written across the top of it, and that accounts for the basic rate of income tax. The shareholder only has to worry about higher rates of tax, and he can get a repayment of that tax credit if he is not liable to income tax at all. If the shareholder is another company, then the dividend is not taxed any further in the hands of the recipient company.

What about salaries?

In a company you pay yourself a salary, which is taxable in your hands, so it is a deduction as far as the company is concerned. From the point of view of the company, directors' salaries and bonuses are an allowable deduction because they are going to be taxed in the hands of the recipient.

One important aspect now is that dividend payments do *not* attract NI contributions whereas salary and bonuses do and these can be quite costly. Where the shareholders and directors of a company are one and the same, it may be worth paying out a part of their 'reward' by way of dividend instead of remuneration. Where the company is paying corporation tax at the 25 per cent rate, this change makes no effective difference to its tax position, but could lead to a useful saving of NI contributions.

There are a number of other factors however; the timing of tax payments, effect on pension scheme contributions and social security benefits, valuation of the company's shares – all these factors need to be taken into consideration. Each situation needs to be looked at on its own merits and professional advice is strongly recommended before any decision is taken.

What are capital allowances?

Capital allowances can also be deducted from trading income provided they have been incurred before the end of the accounting period. While you are not allowed to deduct depreciation in arriving at your taxable income, you are allowed to deduct capital allowances. These are given on a wide range of capital expenditure, for example, plant and machinery, industrial and agricultural buildings, with special treatment available for 'short-life' assets. In some cases, it does not matter whether the asset is in use or not provided that the expenditure has been incurred, the business will qualify for relief.

Allowances on plant and machinery

There has never been a definition of plant and machinery but the term encompasses not only machines, but also many fixtures and fittings, office equipment and motor vehicles.

In recent years the allowances available on plant and machinery have been changed substantially. For expenditure incurred on and after 1 April 1986, the only allowance generally available is a 25 per cent 'writing down' allowance. This is given on the 'pool' of expenditure calculated on a reducing balance basis. Expenditure on new assets is added to the pool and the sole proceeds of plant disposed of is deducted from the pool so as to arrive at the amount on which the 25 per cent allowance is given. If the accounting period is less than 12 months, the allowance is reduced accordingly.

Special treatment is given to motor-cars costing more than £8,000: the writing down allowance on each such car is limited to a maximum of £2,000 a year.

Allowances on industrial buildings

If you buy an industrial building or have it built for use in your own trade or to lease to someone else in their trade, then, you may be entitled to capital allowances on the building. That amount of allowance will depend on whether the building is new or second-hand when you acquired it. If the building is new, then with effect from 1 April 1986 you may claim an annual 'writing down' allowance of 4 per cent on the cost of the building, but not the land. If you buy a second-hand building, you may be entitled to 'writing down' allowances but the level of these will depend upon the allowances claimed by the vendor of the building. If you buy a new commercial building in an Enterprise Zone, you are entitled to an initial allowance of 100 per cent; you need not claim this allowance in full; instead, should you wish, you can claim a 25 per cent 'straight line' allowance on the balance in subsequent years.

If you sell an industrial building, part or even all of the allowances you have claimed may be clawed back, i.e. added to your income, depending upon the price you receive for the building and when the expenditure in respect of which the allowances were claimed was originally incurred.

What is a close company?

Most small companies will be what are known as 'close companies', defined as being controlled by five or fewer shareholders or by any number of directors who are also shareholders. The vast majority of companies in this country are close companies. Bearing in mind that you can still pay 40 per cent tax on your own income, it would be very handy to put some money into a company and leave it to grow, knowing that the bulk of it will never pay more than 25 per cent tax.

The Inland Revenue was aware of this dodge of using companies as money boxes to hold cash that would have been paying tax at fairly high rates as individuals' income.

Until the 1987 Budget the Revenue had the power to apportion the income of companies to shareholders. However, due to a case heard in the Court of Appeal in 1986 this has been amended. The 1989 Budget abolished the close company apportionment of investment income for accounting periods beginning on or after 1 April 1989. As a result, income will no longer be taxed on the individuals. Instead, there will be a 40 per cent CT charge on close investment companies which retain most of their profit.

Furthermore, if your company pays tax at 25 per cent, then you do not want to take the money out of the company and pay tax on it. You just borrow it from the company and carry on borrowing larger and larger amounts and never pay back the sums borrowed. But the Revenue have spotted this loophole too. Now, when a shareholder receives such a loan, the company has to put on deposit with the Collector of Taxes the equivalent of ACT so the loan is treated virtually as a dividend. In addition, the recipient could be assessed to income tax on the benefit of the loan. The annual benefit would be equal to the amount of deemed interest on the loan at the rate of 14.5 per cent.

There are stringent new rules under the Directors and Insolvency Act 1985 which have particular relevance for close companies and their directors–shareholders. Under this Act anyone who acts as a director is considered to be a director and is personally liable for any debts arising should the company continue to trade while insolvent. (The definition of director includes shadow directors, non-executive directors, etc.) The Act does not allow for the excuse of incompetence or lack of knowledge, and assumes that directors must be responsible for their actions and those of their companies. In certain circumstances directors can be jointly and severally liable for the actions of fellow directors. Financial implications aside, should a director fail to fulfil the administrative obligations as laid out in the Companies Act and the Insolvency Act 1986, fines as well as imprisonment can be enforced. Directors can also be disqualified from acting as a director for up to 15 years. Careful study of this Act is therefore advised.

Value added tax

You do not charge VAT unless your annual turnover exceeds £23,600. It is important to register promptly when you realise that you are liable to exceed this amount in a year or £8,000 in two consecutive preceding quarters. The VAT inspector will want tax on your sales from the date of your registration. If you do not register in time, he will still want to collect tax from the date you should have registered, and will not allow you to set off the VAT on expenses incurred during the intervening period.

It is possible to register voluntarily. This is particularly useful if you make mainly zero-rated supplies because it enables you to get back the VAT you have paid out. Most supplies attract VAT at the standard rate of 15 per cent but certain categories are zero-rated, i.e. there is no VAT payable, and these include most foods, books and newspapers, transport, heating fuels and children's clothing. The only person who suffers VAT, and this is the usual peculiar approach of most tax legislation, is someone who is exempt from it. It might be the ordinary citizen, or someone in the property business, or bankers, but whoever is exempt cannot reclaim VAT despite having paid it out.

Companies register separately, and if they are part of a group or commonly controlled they can register together. For unincorporated businesses it is the proprietor of the business who has to register and all his business activities are looked at together. So if he has a turnover of £12,500 a year on a fruit stall in the local market and another £13,500 as a consultant, then he must charge VAT on the lot as it is over the £23,600 limit. This does mean keeping records and in recognition of this there are special schemes available to small traders.

In 1986 the government asked HM Customs and Excise to look at ways in which small businesses could reduce their administrative burden when dealing with central government. These recommendations were examined by the Chancellor who in his March 1987 Budget speech announced further proposed changes.

The major change to affect businesses is payment of VAT due on a cash accounting system. This optional system will benefit businesses which have a turnover of up to £250,000 per year. Late payment of invoices in the past has left small businesses with an extremely vulnerable cash flow situation. Now these businesses will not have to pay VAT until the related invoices have been paid.

In addition, there is also an optional annual accounting for VAT, again up to an annual turnover limit of £250,000. Under this scheme, businesses have to complete only one VAT return per year; however, there will be nine *advance* payments on account to be made.

The period regarding registration for VAT purposes has been extended from 10 days to 30 days.

The proposal for compulsory deregistration of small businesses for VAT has been dropped.

VAT: an outline

— VAT is charged by most businesses on all sales and the tax collected is paid over to HM Customs and Excise quarterly. A business can usually claim a set-off for VAT which it has paid. Small businesses may not be liable to register, but this means that they cannot recover it either.

— A business is liable to register for VAT if its sales will exceed £23,600 in a year, or if they have exceeded £8,000 in the past three months. Liability cannot be avoided by failing to register if these limits are exceeded, and VAT suffered cannot be recovered until a business is registered.

— Most supplies attract VAT at the standard rate of 15 per cent for 'zero-rated' or 'exempt' categories. Exports of goods and many supplies of services to foreigners are also zero-rated as well as those goods previously mentioned. Where a supply is zero-rated no VAT is charged, but the business can still recover all the VAT it pays.

— Where a business is exempt – the major ones are property investment, banking and insurance services – VAT is not charged but the business cannot recover VAT which it pays.

- Where the turnover limits are not likely to be exceeded, a business can, in certain circumstances, still register. This may be advantageous, particularly if supplies are being made to other taxable businesses which can recover VAT charged. It is only by registering that the VAT paid can be recovered.
- Individual companies must register separately for VAT, unless they are part of a group or under common ownership, but unincorporated businesses are registered in the name of the proprietors. Thus all businesses run by the same proprietor must be aggregated when considering the registration limits.
- Where a business intends to make sales subject to VAT at some time in the future, it may be allowed to register as an 'intending trader' (subject to certain conditions imposed by Customs and Excise) so as to be able to recover VAT on its expenses in the meantime.
- It is also possible for a newly registered business to reclaim VAT on goods bought prior to registration where these are still held at that time and on services supplied to it for up to six months prior to registration.
- You should be aware that VAT on certain expenses is not recoverable: the most notable example is entertaining customers or suppliers and the cost of buying (but not running) motor cars.
- Registration for VAT requires extra record-keeping, but this should not be significant unless the business is using one of the special schemes for antiques and certain second-hand goods under which VAT is only charged on the margin between cost and selling price, and not on the whole selling price. There are also a variety of schemes for calculating the VAT liability of a retail business.

As the repayment of VAT can handicap the entrepreneur starting off in business when compiling sales forecasts it is advisable, should it show that the VAT limit is going to be exceeded, to allow for the relevant amounts of VAT in the overall forecast. Forewarned is forearmed. Leaflets on VAT can be obtained from your local Customs and Excise office.

What tax choices do you have?

For the sole trader

Let us suppose that you are in a fortunate position in that your pre-tax profits after capital allowances and all the other things (but not remuneration for yourself, as you are not incorporated) are £70,000. Let us take the example of a small businessman who is married. As a sole trader he is entitled to the married man's allowance. In 1989/90 he pays income tax of £22,995.40, Class 2 contributions of £221 and Class 4 contributions of £746.55. His total contribution to the Exchequer is £23,741.95.

For the partnership

If he formed or was part of a partnership, our businessman could take his wife into equal partnership and elect to have her earned income taxed separately. If this is done they would each earn £35,000 worth of income. He will now not get the married man's allowance but both will get the single person's allowance. They would each pay income tax of £9,631.40, Class 4 contributions of £746.55 and Class 2 contributions of £221. Payment by each to the Exchequer would be £10,598.95, the total for both is £21,197.90, which shows a reduction of £2,544.05 when compared to our sole trader example above. For the separate earnings election to be useful, for 1989/90 the couple must have joint incomes (before deduction of allowances and reliefs) of £30,511, with the spouse having an income of at least £7,026. However, the wife must genuinely work for the partnership in a capacity likely to earn the sum of money being paid.

If you are starting a business, never set up as a

husband and wife; make sure that one or other is an employee for the first year. The reason is that you pay income tax on the profits of the preceding year, but when you start out of course, these are non-existent. Your first year's accounts usually form the basis of assessment for the first three tax years. The earnings of an employee are only taxed in one year so if one of you is an employee for that first year you pay tax on those earnings once, but the employer gets the deduction two and a half to three times over. Often it is the husband who sets up on his own and takes the wife as the employee and then the wife is introduced as a partner at the end of the first year.

Table 7.5. Income tax

	Tax rate %	1989/90 band £
Basic rate band	**25**	**20,700**
Higher rate band	**40**	**20,701+**
		£
Personal allowances:		
married		**4,375**
single		**2,785**
wife's earned income allowance		**2,785**

For the company

Let us suppose our married couple choose to incorporate and form a limited company. The company has £70,000 of taxable profits before they draw anything out of their business to live on. Let us assume they each take a salary of £20,000. Income tax on that for 1989/90 works out at £4,303.75, Class 1 NI is £1,364.48 from each employee plus the company's contribution per employee of £2,090: a total contribution per individual of £5,668.23. The company is going to pay 25 per cent on what is left, so if we started off with £70,000 we are going to take away from that two lots of £20,000 as salary. The employer's NI counts as a deduction against profits and that comes out at £4,180. So they are paying on profits of £25,820 at 25 per cent, which is £6,455. The total contribution to the Exchequer is £21,971.46 against £21,197.90 for the partnership, albeit that they have less disposable income, having left some of it in the company.

Benefits in kind ('perks')

One of the advantages of the company structure is that it is possible to provide employees (in particular the directors) with various tax efficient benefits in kind. These are likely to give rise to some additional tax on the individual, based on the value of the benefit that he receives, but the cost of this is likely to be significantly less to him than if he had to provide this benefit entirely at his own expense.

A particularly popular form of 'perk' is the company car. Here the benefit is measured by reference to scales laid down by the Inland Revenue depending on the age, size and value of the car. Currently these range from a benefit for a car of under four years of £1,400 for a car of 1400cc or less and up to £6,150 for a car costing more than £29,000. These amounts are reduced for cars more than four years old or where the individual does more than 18,000 business miles in a year, but is increased if his business mileage is less than 2,500 a year. An additional charge scale applies where the company petrol is supplied for private use.

Remember that the actual cost to the employee is the tax on these scale charges.

Pensions

Pensions can make all the difference to you whether you are self-employed or not.

Personal pensions schemes came into force on 1 July 1988. These schemes are available to both employees and self-employed. Unlike its predecessor, i.e. retirement annuities, the employer will be able to contribute to personal pensions (known as PPSs). Our couple could normally pay only up to 17.5 per cent of their relevant earnings into a pension scheme, though this can be increased for people born in 1954 or earlier. But the company could pay much higher contributions (subject to Inland Revenue approval) and so reduce the CT charge correspondingly. However, if you are going to start a pension scheme you have got to be sure you want it in addition to finding the cash to pay for it.

Let us look at the finances. Take a man aged 53 with a salary of £15,000 out of his one-man-band company. He wants to retire at 60 with a tax-free lump sum of one and a half times his final salary and a pension thereafter of two-thirds of his final salary or a reduced pension in view of the lump sum. The annual contribution for the next seven or eight years could be as high as £54,000 simply because of the applicant's age. The older you are, the higher the premiums become for the same amount of money.

There are a number of special schemes now and it is advisable to contact your independent insurance consultant to find out the most suitable one for you. Your decision, however, should rest on commercial principles rather than on purely tax considerations. Changes were recently announced by the Chancellor to uplift the total benefits upon retirement up to a maximum of £90,000 lump sum payment of 25 per cent of the fund.

There is somewhat of a 'pensions revolution' starting to take place and it should be priority to find out how it affects you. Telegraph Publications publish a pensions guide; this book is available through bookshops or directly from the Telegraph.

Conclusion

Now that the corporation tax rate for small companies has been reduced to 25 per cent, equivalent to the basic rate of income tax, tax alone should not be a reason to stop you from incorporating the business. But you have to remember that if you do this you will have to have an annual statutory audit which entails paying an audit fee. Generally speaking, the running costs of a limited liability company are higher than those of a trading business, and this should be borne in mind. And although it is called a limited liability company, you may not get the full benefit of limited liability because nobody will advance a small company money unless the director-shareholders put up personal guarantees.

You should also remember that as the company and its shareholders are separate legal entities, a double charge to capital gains tax can arise if the shareholders wish to realise the assets in the company. Firstly, there may be a charge within the company to corporation tax on the gain arising on the disposal of the assets concerned by the company. Secondly, there may be a further charge to capital gains tax on the gain arising to the shareholders when they realise their shares, for example, on liquidating the company.

On the other hand, where an individual disposes of his business or sells his shares in his family trading company when he is over 60 or is obliged to retire under that age through ill health, he may be able to claim substantial relief, up to as much as £125,000, against the chargeable gains arising on him in this way.

Corporation tax: an outline

— A company managed in the UK is liable on income and on capital gains.
— The full rate of corporation tax is: year ending 31 March 1986, 40 per cent; year ending 31 March 1987, 35 per cent; year ending 31 March 1988, 35 per cent and year ended 31 March 1989, 35 per cent.
— In 1989/90 a small company with income of up to £150,000 pays tax at 25 per cent. The next £600,000 of profits is effectively taxed at 37.5 per cent. (These limits are reduced if there are associated companies.)
— Capital gains are effectively taxed at 25 per cent for small companies and for large at 35 per cent.
— Tax is normally payable nine months after the end of the accounting period.

— The company is not liable to income tax, so any tax deducted is either offset against liability or repaid.

The imputation system

This is the present system relating to distributed and undistributed profits.

— A company pays tax at the appropriate rate on its profits. When it pays a dividend, it pays advance corporation tax (ACT) at 27/73rds of the dividend for 1987/88 and 25/75ths for 1989/90.
— This can, within limits, be set against the CT liability of that period; any surplus not relieved in this way can be carried forward indefinitely for relief against the CT liability arising in later years, or carried back for up to six years for setting off against the liability of those earlier years.
— The shareholder is entitled to a tax credit equal to the ACT paid over.

Calculation of taxable profits

— All income and gains are assessed on a current year basis.
— Trading income is computed on an accruals or earnings basis.
— Non-trading income (e.g. interest) is usually taxed on a receipts basis and interest paid (other than bank interest) is allowed on a payment basis.
— Capital gains are taxed in the period in which the asset is sold.

Capital allowances

— Capital allowances are being reduced as corporation tax falls. A percentage of the expenditure on certain assets is deductible from taxable profits in the year the expense is incurred.
— Annual writing down allowances are given of 25 per cent on the reducing balance for plant, and 4 per cent on cost on industrial buildings but not the land. The writing down allowance for expensive cars is limited to £2,000 a year.

— Changes have been made with effect from 1 April 1986 to other minor capital allowances.

Relief for trading losses

— These can be set against other income or chargeable gains of the same or the preceding accounting year.
— Relief can be carried forward against future trading profits on the same trade.
— On cessation of trade the losses of the last 12 months can be carried back against trading profits of the three previous years.

Capital gains

— The gains on the disposal of business assets can be deferred if another business asset is acquired with the proceeds though normally not more than one year earlier or three years later.
— Capital losses can be set off against capital gains in the same accounting period, and net losses can be carried forward to future periods.
— Capital losses cannot be set against income.

Close companies

— Broadly speaking, this is a company controlled by directors or five or fewer shareholders. For accounting periods on or after 1 April 1989 the close company apportionment of investment income was abolished. Consequently, income tax is no longer applied on the directors or shareholders, instead CT at 40 per cent is charged to the company.

Conclusion

The different types of taxation dealt with in this chapter must be considered separately, and unless the businessman has a financial background, it would be advisable for him to discuss the implications with his accountant *before* he starts trading. The Daily Telegraph publish a series of tax guides specifically aimed at small businesses, whether or not they are trading as limited companies or self-employed.

Before the reduction in the level of corporation tax, many companies considered their accounts in the light of how much tax they would have to pay rather than from sound business principles. This has changed and will, in all likelihood, continue to change. None of us likes paying tax; the small businessman finds it unrewarding to work all hours only to have his hard-earned money taken away by the taxman. If it makes it easier, consider that if you were not earning money you would not be liable for tax.

8 Planning for tax and using the incentives

The small business entrepreneur is currently fashionable in government circles, and a number of schemes have been introduced to make life easier for him. A summary at the end of this chapter lists the more recent changes and incentives. This chapter also looks at planning for tax and lists a number of relevant points which need to be taken into consideration. It cannot be stressed too strongly that for sole traders and partnerships, as no two personal situations are ever the same, consultation with your tax consultant is essential. The other section in this chapter looks at the effectiveness of some of the government schemes and introduces you to some key questions you ought to be asking yourself, whether as a new business or as an investor. Chapter 7 has already explained the possible benefits and drawbacks of the graduated tax rates, and the dangers of getting caught in the marginal relief band. It has also pointed out the pitfalls for the small company which has not as yet registered for VAT of forgetting to do so.

Initial costs

If you are going to start a new business you will spend money on printing, advertising, legal fees and perhaps rental of an office or of a factory. The incentive for the small business is that your expenses for up to five years before you trade (provided that those expenses would have been allowable had you started to trade) will be allowable against tax on commencement.

Table 8.1 Which form of business should I choose?

	Sole trader/ partnership	**Company**
General	unlimited liability	limited liability (but note possibility of personal guarantees by directors). Also note the stipulations laid out in the Insolvency Act 1986 with regard to directors' liabilities and responsibilities
	statutory audit not required	statutory audit required
	annual returns need not be submitted or statutory books kept	annual returns must be submitted and statutory books kept
	no legal continuity on death	legal continuity
	no restrictions on drawings from business	company law in general prohibits loans to directors. Share capital may only be withdrawn: (a) in the winding up of the company, or (b) where there is a reduction in the company's share capital sanctioned by the courts, or (c) where the company buys back its own shares under the arrangements allowed under the Companies Act 1981 and the Finance Act 1982 (see below).
Taxation		
	income tax charged at rates from 25 per cent to 40 per cent depending on profits	corporation tax for small companies 25 per cent. This tax increases as a company grows and depends on profits. At present the top rate is 35 per cent

'preceding year' basis of assessment (except in opening and closing years of trading)	'actual' basis of assessment
lower total NI contributions (but lesser benefits)	higher total NI contributions (but better benefits) by company as well as directors if employees
relief for personal pension premiums	relief for personal pension premiums
single charge to capital gains tax on disposal of assets	possible double charge to capital gains tax on disposal of assets and subsequent withdrawal of capital, e.g. on liquidation
no capital duty on formation	capital duty payable on formation
interest relief on money borrowed to invest in business, as capital or as a loan	interest relief to individuals only on to money borrowed to invest in company as share capital or by way of a loan

Which structure is best?

There is no golden rule about which particular form of business structure is best. They all have to be individually examined and applied to your personal circumstances; Table 8.1 summarises the main differences.

Previously, the main reason for setting up as a company was that it gave you the benefit of limited liability, which meant that should the company fail then the creditors of that company could only go as far as the company and not into your home. However, the new Act has adjusted directors' responsibilities and the limited liability reason is now not a practical one. You could find that the bank will not lend a new business any money unless you give them a personal guarantee, and possibly security on your home which again negates forming a limited company.

The difference between a sole trader and a partnership from a tax point of view is small; whether you are a sole trader or partnership depends on whether you are going into business on your own or with somebody else. The costs of running this sort of operation are considerably less than those incurred when running a company. The main additional expense of running a company is probably the audit fee. On the other hand, as a sole trader or partnership you will certainly need to have accounts prepared to send to the tax inspector and these may well also be required by the bank in the case of a loan or large overdraft; in any case properly prepared accounts must be an important ingredient in the management of your business. The other costs which you can incur in a company that you do not have in a partnership or as a sole trader are those arising out of certain statutory obligations imposed in the running of the company: having meetings, keeping statutory books, sending in the annual return to be registered at Companies House and so on.

It is also generally easier to draw money, as a direct loan, from a sole trader's business or from a partnership. Let us say you are a director of a company. Now it is generally contrary to company law to take money out of a company as a loan, so if you want to draw money out it has got to be by way of salary or bonus. If you take it out in this way you have got to deduct PAYE. Within an established sole trader or partnership you can have drawings throughout the year and pay the tax later and in two stages.

Let us look at the typical person these days who is starting in business having been made redundant and who has received a redundancy payment of, perhaps, £20,000. To get into business, he will have to spend, let us say £10,000 on capital equipment: plant and machinery, fixtures and fittings. After the first 12 months most businesses might even make a loss; however, let us say that he does quite well and comes out even, therefore no profit or loss. But he needs to take some money out of the business to live on, and let us say he takes £6,000 out.

If it was a company, it would have made a loss of £6,000 because he paid himself a salary of that amount and all he can do is carry it forward and set it off against future profits. He has actually paid some tax – PAYE on the salary of £6,000.

As a sole trader, his drawings of £6,000 do not count as salary; he is just drawing in advance of profits, although he has not made any. All he has done is break even. If, however, he has made a loss in this first period, apart from his drawings, then he can carry that loss back for three years into all his prior earnings. In fact, this relief is available for trading losses in the first four years of business. If he paid tax during those years he may therefore be able to recover it up to the level of the losses incurred, provided he is operating as a sole trader or in a partnership. In a company, it would cost him the PAYE and NI on £6,000 which might amount to, say, £1,000.

An employer has to pay higher NI contributions in respect of his employees, including the directors of his company. It does cost a bit more, but on the other hand the employee gets better benefits out of those contributions. If you are operating as a company you can generally set up better personal pension arrangements than as a sole trader or partnership.

The tax rules about converting a sole trader or partnership into a company can be quite complex, particularly as regards the timing of the change.

New rules apply on the assessment of partnerships taking place after 19 March 1985, where no continuation election is made. The partnership will be assessed for each of the first four years on actual profits arising during that period with the previous years basis operating for the fifth and subsequent year. This rule applies only to established partnerships not to newly set up ones.

In practice you may find that large suppliers prefer to do business with a limited company rather than with a sole trader or partnership; therefore some commercial pressure may be brought to bear on the need to incorporate. All these aspects should be kept under constant review in collaboration with your accountant.

Tax planning

This subject has never been more important than now. The progressive reduction of the rates of corporation tax through to 31 March 1988 means that the deferment of corporate tax liabilities will be a certain means of saving tax. This section does no more than indicate areas which may be worth examining more closely. The operation of the tax system, company law and practice in all these areas is complex and once again it is essential that professional advice is taken when looking at particular situations.

Year-end planning

The planning for the review of a company's tax position should take place well before the year end as part of an ongoing programme involving directors and advisers. Areas for consideration include:

1. Hire purchase; claim capital allowances on full cash price.
2. Lease or buy? Can the business absorb the full capital allowances? How do interest rates compare on a lease contract and bank borrowing?
3. Rent or buy? Again, can the business absorb full capital allowances? Consider the impact of industrial building allowances and the 'machinery' element in buildings.
4. Are your investments tax efficient? What is the best use of surplus funds?

Salaries and dividends

It used to be accepted that for tax purposes salary was preferable to dividend, but there are further points which need consideration before a decision is made: these are listed below.

1. Salaries in excess of the justifiable commercial level may be challenged by the Inland Revenue. Not generally a problem except where directors' wives are employed with no real duties.
2. The aim should be to raise directors' remuneration

up to a level where the individual's marginal rate of income tax at least equates to the company's marginal rate of corporation tax. This can be achieved by fixing bonus payments after the year end.
3. PAYE on remuneration may be due for payment over to the Inland Revenue earlier than the company's corporation tax liability. A cash flow problem may be avoided or reduced by providing for payment of the bonus (as noted in the above point) some time after the balance sheet date. However, remember that PAYE is due when the individual is able to draw down against his bonus entitlement, *not* when he actually does.
4. Where the individual draws advances against future bonus payments, the Revenue may assess 'deemed ACT' (repayable) with interest on such 'loans' or make a benefit on the basis that it is a 'free loan'. Where the individual is a director, such advances may be in breach of company law.
5. Impact on NI contributions.

Fringe benefits

Although legislation is much tighter now, scope still exists for providing directors and higher paid employees with various forms of non-cash benefits. There are a number of points to remember, not least of which is the wide definition of the word 'director'.

Earnings thresholds for 'higher paid' employees earning over £8,500 per annum include:

— all salaries as generally understood;
— value of all benefits received;
— all expenses reimbursed before any allowable deductions.

Various perks also have a measure of taxable benefit, such as living accommodation and company cars.

Pension schemes

Although at present pension schemes offer the best opportunity for tax planning which will benefit both the company and its employees in all categories, currently the main advantages of an approved occupational pension scheme are the substantial tax reliefs and exemptions that are allowed, particularly in the payment of tax-free lump sums on retirement or on death in service.

Purchase of own shares

Under the 1981 Companies Act, companies were given the power to purchase their own shares. Under the 1982 Finance Act, tax relief was introduced to enable unquoted trading companies to make such purchases without undue cost in terms of tax. This means that the shareholder who is selling his shares can treat the sale as a normal capital gains tax disposal, with no tax charges payable by the company. Where relief does not apply, cash passing from company to shareholder must be treated as an income distribution, with advanced corporation tax payable by the company, and possibly a higher rate liability on the shareholder.

There are a number of stringent requirements that have to be satisfied, but this is a route that may well be worth examining when an investor in the company wishes to realise some or all of his investment and there is no market readily available.

What type of capital is best?

Whether you use bank money or not depends on whether you can get it from the bank. If you have the money to put in the business yourself, and if you can make a good profit, why give some of it to the bank? You may feel you need extra money. While under-capitalising is a mistake, at the same time you may not wish to get tied up with interest payments on borrowed money. On the other hand, you may prefer to keep at least some of your personal capital outside the business in case of emergency.

The question of how much money you should put into the business by way of share capital (in the case of a company), and by way of a loan – in other words, your own money, not outside finance – should be decided on commercial factors. It is something which you will need to go into with your advisers at the time. A guideline is that you ought to have sufficient share capital invested to make the company look a reasonably substantial operation. Table 8.2 sets out the options.

In Chapter 1 we briefly covered the government incentive schemes which are available, and here we look at the Business Expansion Scheme (BES). If you as an individual invest money in a business under the BES you can get income tax relief for the money put in during the year in which you invested it. After 5 April 1987, the Chancellor proposed to reduce the 'bunching' of investments provided that

(a) the investment must be made in the first half of the tax year (between 6/4 and 5/10);

(b) to carry back up to a maximum of £5,000 in respect of the total BES investment made in this period. However, this option will apply to investment made after 5 April 1987. Remember, this can only be exercised upon claiming the relief. The Chancellor has also relaxed the BES rules on investment in film production companies. And investments in residential property letting companies now also qualify under the BES rules.

Let us take an example. You are thinking of investing in the BES and are going to put in the maximum of £40,000. (As of the 1988 Budget, a company cannot raise more than £500,000 in a BES in any year. However, for private rented housing – and ship chartering – the amount is £5 million.) If you are paying tax at 40 per cent of your income, you can set this investment off against your income and get tax relief at 40 per cent.

One of the rules of this game is that you have to keep the investment in for five years. Let us assume that you do leave the investment for five years and that it doubles in value. On actual cost your investment will have gone up from £16,000 (after tax relief) to £80,000 – a 500 per cent increase – so this is quite an incentive; what is more, for investments made after 18 March 1986 there will be no capital gains tax to pay on this profit. But there are restrictions. Firstly, the amount of investment cannot

Table 8.2 Share capital or loan capital?

	Share capital	Loan capital
Tax relief on payment of dividends/interest	No, but ACT may be credited against the company's corporation tax liability	Yes
Voting rights and a say in the running of the company	Yes	No
Right to participate in profits	Yes	No
Receipts of dividends/ interest taxable	Yes	Yes
Can be issued at a discount	No	Yes
Dividend/interest payable if the company is making a loss	No	Yes
Easy to reduce share/loan capital	No	Yes
Tax relief if share/loan capital not paid	Yes	Yes/No

be more than £40,000 in any one year, although this can be spread over a number of different investments. Secondly, you have got to keep the shares for five years and if you sell them in the meantime, you will lose any relief already given although there may be a limited concession in certain circumstances. Thirdly, and this is one of the key points, the company that you are investing in has to be completely independent from you, the investor. This means that neither you nor any 'associates' (broadly speaking, parents, grandparents, children, more distant relatives or partners) can have a controlling interest in the company, nor can you or any such associate be an employer or paid director of the company. Fourthly, the company must be a single unquoted company or the holding unquoted company of a group, for example, you cannot invest in an ICI subsidiary. Fifthly, it must exist wholly or substantially for the purpose of carrying on trade in the UK. And lastly, it is limited to certain types of business; among the types excluded are farming, property development and financial services.

An individual may make the investment directly or through one of a number of 'approved investment funds' which have been set up by some banks and stockbrokers. These schemes seek to attract investment funds from individuals and place them in qualifying businesses. Investments made through these funds qualify for full income tax relief, but only when the fund actually makes the investment in the company concerned (see section on Legislation for further details).

Benefit for the investor

Borrowed money

It is no longer necessary to work in partnerships or companies in order to get relief from money that you borrow to put into them. This helps a retired partner who wants to leave in some money he has borrowed from the bank – he can now get tax relief on that money, provided he is active in the management of the business. Since the 1982 Budget you have been able to claim relief, even if you have less than 5 per cent interest.

Using company losses

If unquoted companies in which you have invested lose money and you make a loss, you can set that loss off against your other income. Of course, the last thing you want to do when you are entering into an investment is think about what happens if you lose it.

Incentive for corporate investment

Investment is encouraged in areas of high unemployment and economic decay. This particularly applies to city centres. So far the government has designated a number of such areas, known as Enterprise Zones, throughout the UK. Each zone covers an area of about 1,200 acres. The incentives to set up business in these Enterprise Zones are considerable. There is a 100 per cent allowance on any money that you spend on new or improved buildings, including office and commercial property (i.e. it is not just limited to industrial buildings, as is generally the case with these allowances). You will be exempt from general rates on industrial and commercial property. There will be a relaxation of the planning rules and of the industrial training boards' controls. You will, however, have to comply with limited requests from government for statistical information.

The government has also introduced a useful allowance for companies enabling them to claim against tax the costs of raising money, including legal and other fees. Now that capital allowances generally are being less generous, these other allowances are relatively more valuable.

Loss relief for new trades

In order to encourage individuals to set up as a sole trader or in a partnership to carry on a new trade, profession or vocation, where a tax loss arises in either the tax year of commencement or any of the following three years, the loss can be set against the taxpayer's total income for the three previous years (relief is given for the earliest available year first). In certain circumstances, therefore, relief for a trading loss will be given in a tax year before the trade commenced.

Legislation

Legislation designed to ease the burden of taxation on small companies

THE SMALL COMPANIES' RATE: the rate of corporation tax for small companies was reduced from 38 per cent to 30 per cent with effect from 1 April 1983 and further reduced in each consecutive budget to its present level of 25 per cent. The lower rate applies if taxable profits do not exceed £150,000. Marginal relief at an effective rate of 37.5 per cent applies if taxable profits are between £100,000 and £750,000. The normal rate of 35 per cent applies if taxable profits exceed £750,000.

THE REGISTRATION LIMIT FOR VAT: since 14 March 1989, a trader has not needed to register for VAT purposes unless:

— his taxable turnover, at any time during the following 12 months, will exceed £23,600; or
— at the end of a calendar quarter, his taxable turnover has exceeded either £8,000 in the previous quarter or £23,600 in the previous 12 months;
— the time for notification to be registered for VAT has been extended to 30 days.

Registered persons are able to deregister if at any time in the following 12 months their taxable turnover will not exceed £22,100 or they have been registered for two years and their turnover (inclusive of VAT) in each of those years has not exceeded £23,600, and they do not expect their turnover to go above that in the next 12 months. Notification must take place within 30 days if the business is no longer entitled to register. Whether this will be advantageous depends upon the particular circumstances.

In the March 1987 Budget, it was announced that cost accounting and annual accounting systems were proposed. However, the business must have a turnover of under £250,000. These proposals are deemed beneficial for a business's cash flow.

SELF-BILLING: A business raising a self-billed invoice will be responsible for establishing the precise VAT liability. If the invoice is incorrect, HM Customs can issue a notice raising the self-billed invoice and then assess the invoice for the tax due.

Legislation designed to encourage investment in small companies

RELIEF FOR CERTAIN PRE-TRADING EXPENSES: expenditure of a revenue nature which is incurred before trading begins is eligible for relief:

— if it is incurred within five years before trading begins; and if
— it would have been allowed as a deduction for tax purposes if it had been incurred after trading had begun.

Examples of pre-trading expenses which are eligible for relief include rent, rates and employees' wages.

RELIEF FOR INTEREST PAID ON MONEY BORROWED FOR INVESTMENT:

1. Interest relief on borrowing to invest in close companies: an individual has to satisfy one of two conditions before he may be able to obtain any tax relief for interest on funds borrowed in order to invest in or lend to a close company. These are:

(a) he must have a material interest in the company (i.e. greater than 5 per cent of the ordinary share capital); or

(b) he must work for the greater part of his time for the company or an associated company and hold some shares in the company.

2. Interest relief on borrowing to invest in employee-controlled companies: where shares in a company are acquired by its employees so that they obtain control of the company (e.g. an 'employee buy-out'), an individual who borrows money to fund his purchase of shares may be able to obtain tax relief on the interest paid, subject to various conditions being satisfied.

3. Interest relief on borrowing to invest in partnerships: provided that he is a member of the partnership, an individual who borrows money to invest in a partnership, either as capital or as loan, or to buy an interest in the partnership from another partner, e.g. one who is retiring, may be able to obtain tax relief on the interest paid.

INCOME TAX RELIEF FOR CAPITAL LOSSES ON SHARES IN UNQUOTED TRADING COMPANIES: an individual subject to certain conditions, set against his taxable income a capital loss arising on the disposal of shares in an unquoted trading company. This relief does *not* normally apply to the loss of money *lent* to the company.

A claim for the relief may be made for the year immediately following and must be made within two years of the end of the year for which the relief is claimed. Any unused balance of the loss will be available to set against earned income and then against unearned income.

THE BUSINESS EXPANSION SCHEME: the BES is designed to encourage individuals to invest risk capital in new or existing corporate trading enterprises based in the UK, and it provides for income tax relief on amounts up to specified limits when an individual subscribes for newly issued ordinary shares in qualifying companies. Relief is to be given only to unconnected minority investors in the shares of the company concerned.

Initially, the scheme was to have run until April 1987; however, the Chancellor in his 1986 Budget expanded the life of the scheme indefinitely. At present relief is available on investment of amounts of up to £40,000 per person (husband and wife are counted as one) in the year. Relief is given at the taxpayer's top marginal rate of income tax.

Relief is withdrawn (up to the amounts of the sales proceeds) if the shares are disposed of after five years, for shares issued after 18 March 1986, no charge to capital gains tax arises on any profit (and there is no relief for any loss). For shares issued earlier, capital gains tax may be payable where the sale proceeds exceed the original cost before any income tax relief.

Entitlement to the relief is dependent upon the main conditions:

— the individual must qualify by not owning more than 30 per cent of the company;

— the company must qualify by being a UK-based company;
— the shares must be issued to the individual by the company for the purpose of a qualifying trade;
— the shares must be retained for five years;
— certain activities do not qualify, notably farming, property development and financial services;
— chartering of UK-registered ships;
— the individual must not be a paid director.

The 1986 Finance Bill included a power to make further changes, if necessary, to the definition of a 'qualifying trade'.

However, for capital gains arising from disposals after 5 April 1988, the tax is designed to include 'real' rather than 'inflationary' gains. As a result, for disposals taking place on or after 6 April 1988 the base value for CGT purposes has been uplifted to the value of the asset (if held) from the acquired date if that acquired date is on or after 31 March 1982. The tax rate is now linked to the level of income received over the period but the gain will still be under the CGT rules and not the income tax ones. The 1989–90 annual exemption is £5,000 for individuals and £2,500 for most trustees.

Relief is only given if the trade of a company has been carried on for four months or more.

In the 1986 Budget, the Chancellor excluded companies who held goods as an investment and did not actively try to sell them; this included the trading in fine wines and antiques.

RELIEF FOR COSTS OF RAISING BUSINESS LOAN FINANCE: expenditure which has been incurred since April 1980 on the incidental costs of either obtaining or repaying qualifying loan finance is allowed as a deduction in computing the trading profits of a business for tax purposes, or, if appropriate, as a management expense for investment companies. For this purpose incidental costs include, amongst others, fees, commissions, advertising and printing.

In this connection a qualifying loan is defined as being any borrowing which meets either of the two conditions:

(a) the interest on the loan is deductible in computing the trading profits of the business (e.g. bank loan); or
(b) the interest on the loan is treated as a charge on income (e.g. loans from institutions to finance trading).

The relief is extended to the incidental costs of raising convertible loans, provided that the conversion date of such loans is not earlier than three years from the issue of the loan. Any abortive costs of obtaining finance are also deductible if the finance would have been a qualifying loan.

9 Recruitment and employment law

Taking on staff is an important matter and must be dealt with within certain criteria. If you select an applicant wrongly, it can affect the smooth running of your business in financial as well as physical terms. There are three stages of employment: deciding what sort of person you want and what his function will be, then setting out to find that person; interviewing and employing a suitable applicant; and lastly, if your choice proves to be wrong, getting rid of him. None of the above is as simple as it sounds, and in the latter case you obviously have to stay within the law.

The first thing to do is analyse the job you want doing, and then decide what sort of person would fill this role. Once this has been done you must set about finding a suitable applicant, either by yourself, through advertising, or by using an agency (this can be a government agency or a private company). Always be specific in an advertisement or when talking to an agency, mentioning all aspects of the job, the type of applicant you are interested in, the salary and the terms of employment. It is also sensible to reiterate these points during the interview. Depending on the type of position, you may wish to call the applicants back for a second or third interview. A second interview is indeed advisable and you can often gain a deeper understanding of an applicant's character by doing this. Once you have offered an applicant the job this must be confirmed in writing, and by 13 weeks from the date of commencement of the position, he must be given a contract of employment. This leads us on to the last point: termination of employment. If an employee does not have a contract of employment, then difficulties will arise. When you dismiss an employee you must make sure that you stick to the letter of the law.

Taking on staff

There are certain elements that you must be absolutely sure about before you recruit. First ask yourself whether or not other members of your staff could share the workload of this vacancy. If you do need another member of staff then you must write a full job description. This need not be a lengthy document but simply a summary of the main elements of the job and the work to be done. Also take into account the relationship of the job to other tasks being carried out within the work environment. List the tasks in order of performance or importance, looking at the job or department not only from the point of view of the present but also of the future. The amount of detail will obviously vary depending on the type and level of the job concerned. Be specific, as this can avoid confusion and problems over job demarcation at a later date. The specifications must include the type of person you envisage being suitable for the job. All this is time consuming but in the end is absolutely necessary.

If you are advertising the vacancy yourself, make sure that you use the right media for the job category and that the advertisement shows clearly the job title and description. Be careful when writing the copy to see that everything stated is correct, and that you can stand by your printed word which is precisely what the advertisement becomes. Some people, in order to attract applicants, add conditions and benefits which not only can they not meet, but which do not exist. If an applicant starts working for you and then finds out that the job is not as advertised, he has the right to commence legal proceedings against you and stands a good chance of winning.

If you do not want to handle recruitment yourself, then there are a number of organisations to whom you can turn for assistance: which one you choose depends on the position and its inherent duties, in other words, its category. There are local job centres for blue collar staff as well as a government agency for white collar staff. Many private agencies specialise in placing clerical or secretarial staff, while others have executive staff registered with them. All recruitment companies charge fees, based on their range of placement. These can be from 5 per cent to, in some cases, as high as 22 per cent of the applicant's gross per annum starting salary. Do make sure that you know the agency's terms so that you do not discover, after the exercise has been completed, that you have a bill not only for the placement fee but for advertising costs as well. Be specific and tell the agency or job centre the job specification, the type of person you are looking for, and the qualifications, age, etc., that the candidates must have. Remember that merit and ability must always be considered as well as age; theory is no substitute for practice.

Application forms

Whether or not you are using an agency to recruit applicants always make sure that you have a proper application form completed by all candidates (see Figure 9.1). If you are using an agency insist that they submit copies of application forms for all candidates put forward for interview. These forms are valuable documents because they form the basis of staff records, and must be filed away in a private location with strictly limited access. As soon as anyone replies to your advertisement, he should be sent an application form. If it is properly designed, it should have space for you to make notes during an interview. Notes are essential so that you can, if necessary, show subsequently that you are recruiting for the job on capability alone and that you are not exercising discrimination. If you do not do this, it

RECRUITMENT APPLICATION FORM

This information is required in order to assess your suitability for the position applied for. Please endeavour to answer all questions as fully and accurately as possible. Any information supplied will be treated as strictly confidential and no approach will be made to either past or present employers without your consent.

Position applied for   Permanent/Temporary   Company

Surname   Christian Names
Mr./Mrs./Miss/Ms.

Address ____________________

Tel. No.
Home: ____________
Work: ____________

Date of Birth   Place of Birth   Nationality

Current Passport   Yes/No   Expiry Date

Marital Status   No. of Children & Ages

Height Weight	Details of Gen. Health/Serious Illness or Operations

---

House Owner/Tenant

Car Owner

Full Driving Licence   Yes/No   Endorsements

Leisure Activities ____________________

Membership of Societies, Associations etc. (Details of any offices held) ____________

Figure 9.1: Application form

EDUCATION (From Secondary School Level)

From	To	Name of School/College/University	Exams Taken	Results

Any other activities ______

EMPLOYMENT (Present position First)

From	To	Employer's Name/Address and Type of Business	Job Title and Brief Description	Salary Start	Salary Finish	Reasons for Leaving

LENGTH OF NOTICE REQUIRED ______

REFERENCES (Please supply the names and addresses of 3 persons from whom references can be obtained. At least 2 of these should be previous employers).

1. ______________________ 2. ______________________ 3. ______________________

COMMENTS (Any other points you wish to make concerning your application and career ambitions)

SIGNED: DATE:

would be very difficult to prove at a later date that you have not discriminated in filling the vacancy. You need the evidence of your thoughts at the time to show that you assessed the person in the light of the requirements of the job. Notes are important too, when you talk about money. You arrive at the point when you offer a starting salary. Say you offer £6,500 p.a. and the candidate says that he is earning that now, and does not want to move. You respond by saying that in six months' time, you will give him an increase to £7,000 p.a. He accepts and after six months, having looked at his pay packet, he finds that you have not increased his salary. He can then take you to court for breach of contract. Given these circumstances, his word against yours, the chances are he will win. All this is why the application form is important as well as the notes, signed and dated, taken at an interview. This is the only cover you have in the case of one person's word against your own.

Before each interview read through the completed forms and make a note of any questions you need answering, or any clarification which is required. Make sure that the applicants meet the basic qualifications specified in your job description, check that there are no unexplained 'gaps' in their previous career path, that salary requirements fall within your parameters, and that no immediate problems with health or personal circumstances are visible. Check that the candidates have given at least three references, including two from employers (one of which should be current if the person is in employment). After the interview and before offering the job to the favoured applicant, take up references. Do not leave it until after the job has been offered or even until after the person has joined your firm as it is then too late.

It is a good idea to make two check lists before interviewing applicants, the first containing the job description, and the second, general questions you need answering. During the interviews stick to the sequence of your check lists, referring if necessary to your notes. After describing the job fully, ask your questions letting the applicants answer in their own way, with you acting merely as a prompt. By doing interviews in this manner, you will often learn more than by directing a continuous stream of standard questions. Candidates will tell you what they think you want to hear. Seek explanation and clarification to your list of questions, noting the answers. Double check the contents of the application form, i.e. dates, job content and reason for leaving past employment. Talk about leisure interests as this often gives a much greater insight into a person's character.

Remember to prepare for interviews, know exactly the type of person you are looking for and keep control of the interview at all times. Prepare a reasonable schedule so that you are not rushing the interviews, allocating approximately an hour per candidate. Should second or third interviews be needed before a final selection is made, these should be in-depth probes checking professional competence, character strengths and weaknesses, double-checking career ambitions and personal stability.

Selecting applicants

Before you start the interviews you need to know about the law on discrimination. However, as long as you base your selection on capability to do the job and sound business reasons – and can prove that you have done so – you are free to exercise your own judgement. The legislation encourages you to manage.

An example here will help. A woman applied for a job in Nottingham in a men's outfitters and was turned down. In that department a large part of their sales was for trousers and they felt there would be some embarrassment if a lady took inside-leg measurements. It was found to be unfair discrimination because there were seven men assistants who could do this, or alternatively she could ask customers to hold the tape themselves.

Making an offer

It does not matter how full the offer letters are, as long as they are conditional. Put the offer in writing for your own protection, but unless the offer is conditional, the moment it is accepted you have a contract.

Everything on the application form is true from the moment the employee starts work with you. So you can cut out the whole of the section at the end of the form in which the applicants certify that everything on the form is true. This is of no use to you once they have set foot on your premises to start work and are under a contract of employment. The reason is that you had the opportunity to check before they started work with you. The same thing applies to references. They are deemed to have been satisfactory and to have been checked by you before the employee starts. They are no use once employment has commenced. It cost one company £10,000 to get rid of an employee who had been with them for eight working days. The major reason was because his references were unsatisfactory, but by the contract they were held to have been found satisfactory the moment they allowed him to start.

So do make the offer letter conditional, the two things on which it is normally conditional being satisfactory references and medicals.

Rejection letters

You will have to reject some applicants. If you have used an agency, they will do this for you. But if you are sending them yourself, make the letter short and do not go into the reasons for your decision as it can only expose you to problems.

Example

Dear Mr Smith,

Ref.: Vacancy for

Further to your interview on Monday 19 April 1985, with regard to the above vacancy, I regret to advise that on this occasion your application has not been successful.

May I take this opportunity to thank you for your interest shown in our company and wish you every success in your future career.

Yours sincerely,

Contract of employment

It is important to understand what a contract is, and what it is not. The first point is that it does not have to be written down. Let us take an example. If you say to someone: 'Please come at 9 o'clock on Monday morning and start work with me as a Personnel Director' and the invitation is taken up, you will have to pay the going rate for the post of Personnel Director or for anyone on an equal level in the company. You will have to give that person all the pay, privileges and rights that those on that level have – although you have not put anything on paper at all, and have not mentioned the rate of pay or any conditions. That is how easy it is to get into a contract of employment.

One thing your contract of employment is not, is that which was referred to in the Contract of Employment Act 1972. That has nothing to do with the contract of employment at all – it is merely a written statement which you as an employer must produce within 13 weeks. The contract of employment consists of a range of items: it includes anything you put in your advertisement, anything you say at interviews, all notices you may have put on the notice board, any work rules you may have, and any undertakings you may have with your work force.

Remember that it is up to you to get the information right. So if the job centre advertises your vacancy at the wrong salary, and you do not correct it, then you will have to pay the applicant the advertised rate. The advertisement must be worded correctly. There was a very interesting case of a woman in Northern Ireland who answered an advertisement for a shorthand typist. It said all the usual things to sell the job: four weeks' notice, three weeks' leave, good pension arrangements, permanent pensionable employment, luncheon vouchers, etc. As the judge in the case said afterwards, they carried out the interviews impeccably. The woman could have been in no doubt as to what she had to do. Two years later a new boss arrived and after a short time he said, 'I'm sorry but your standard really isn't up to what I require', and he fired her with the proper notice and pay. The woman went straight to the Crown Court. Her employers were found to be in breach of contract, but the interesting thing was how much compensation she received. She was aged 32 when she was fired and was awarded 28 years' salary – to the normal retirement age – plus compensation for the loss of pension. So when you are writing an advertisement, be careful; do not say 'permanent pensionable employment'. Yet many major companies are still making this mistake. As a small business you cannot afford to. One cannot stress too strongly the importance of getting the recruitment procedure right. You may want to attract staff with an enticing advertisement, but do not lose sight of the essentials.

It would be best to ask your solicitor to draw up a standard contract of employment. The contract must include the names of both employer and employee, the date the employment commences, the rate of pay and method of payment, the job title, holiday entitlement, pension rights, sickness pay, hours of work, discipline at work, complaints procedure, and period of notice. There are other items known as 'Code of Practice' and whilst these do not fall within the parameters of the employment laws they are usually taken into account by an industrial tribunal and should for safety be included in the contract. These include opportunities for promotion and training, trade union membership, job flexibility and overtime, and restrictions on future employment (i.e. trade secrets or client lists).

Make sure that the contract of employment is prepared in duplicate and that a second copy, duly signed and dated by the employee, remains on your personnel records together with his application form, letter of offer and your interview notes.

During the course of work

There are certain rights gathered during the term of employment and you can read about these in greater detail in many law guides, but a few are selected here for your information.

Transfer of ownership and businesses have some effect on employees' rights and they need to be told if this is happening. There is also the Social Security and Housing Benefit Act which came into force 1 April 1983. Then it is vital that you follow the requirements of the health and safety legislation. It is the one Act that will have an increasing effect on the office as well as the manufacturing industry. Get all the good advice you can and make sure that you are operating properly. Have a close look at the office yourself. Let us take two examples. If you have plugs that are flush with the floor, or if you are running a calculator and typewriter or light all off the same plug, you should beware. If your filing cabinets do not have the proper safety device to ensure that only one drawer can be opened at a time, then again beware. You are unsafe and therefore liable.

Working with the trade unions

As with all discussion or presentation, it is important to keep a clear head and a calm temperament. And, as stressed earlier in a different context, it is the first agreement you come to, whether on representation rights or negotiation rights, which is the most important. For example, in the engineering industry, a trade union agreement remained in force from before World War I up until 10 years or so ago.

As an employer there is always the temptation to be as polite and helpful as possible and agree to see the trade union officials. As soon as you start dealing with the trade union you may in effect be recognising the union and, if so, then you must take account of their obligations imposed on you. For example, if you do recognise a union for collective bargaining and if a shop steward is appointed, then he is entitled to reasonable time off for trade union duties and activities

(Employment Protection (Consolidation) Act 1978). You would also have an obligation to keep the union informed on any new company projects, and to consult it about any redundancy. Normally this should not be too much of a problem but it can lead to lengthy delays.

Inevitably in the course of company life there are going to be problems: somebody will have to be disciplined, or sacked, the company may also hit hard times. You could face the risk of an allegation of unfair dismissal and the onus will be on you to prove that the dismissal was fair and legal – tribunals can be a costly business so do take all the necessary precautions. (Booklet No. 13, *Unfairly Dismissed*, can be obtained from the Department of Employment.)

Before recognising a union or dealing with the local trade union official, stop and ask your employees what they want. If you find that people are not sure about whether they want to be members of a union, give them time to think things through. If the majority want to be members of a particular union, and want that union to negotiate their terms and conditions for them, then you can decide what to do about entering into some sort of recognition of that trade union. Employees have the following rights regarding union membership:

— Not to be dismissed for proposing or being members of an independent trade union or for attending union activities at an appropriate time (lunch times, outside working hours, at previously agreed times);
— Not to have action taken against them by the employer to stop them from belonging to a union – this is legally known as 'action short of dismissal';
— Not to be chosen for redundancy because they belong to a union.

If your company has a closed shop arrangement, then legally employees cannot be dismissed or made redundant for not belonging to a union. They also cannot be compelled to become union members.

There is no legal right to recognise a union.

However, there are possible advantages to be gained from trade union representation.

If you should have problems in employee relations, remember that the majority of ACAS's negotiations are on behalf of small and medium-sized companies. It is recommended that you obtain all the necessary booklets on individual rights of employees and trade union law from the Department of Employment.

The 1982 and 1984 Employment Acts introduced a number of changes. The 1982 Act prohibits companies or authorities from recognising the previous 'union labour only requirements': this benefits the non-union businesses – small firms and self-employed people – when tendering for contracts. It also has taken away the legal immunity which previously protected trade unions and individuals who organised or threatened to organise action against the employers in the hope of trying to impose their own requirements. Now a company can seek an injunction against the union, or the individual, to restrain them from unlawful acts, and to sue them for damages. It also specifies the number of union members who may legally demonstrate outside their place of work and prohibits the use of secondary picketing. There is a booklet which can be obtained from job centres entitled, *Industrial action and the law*.

Sickness

On 14 June 1982 doctors stopped providing medical certificates for sickness of less than seven days. You should install your own departmental or company system to control any form of absenteeism by means of written reason for absence from the employee (formally known as self-certification). Be aware that part of your contract may not be enforceable now because you can no longer ask for doctors' certificates after two or three days.

The change means that you must now pay sickness benefit (Statutory Sick Pay) for the first six weeks of illness, but only during the times when the employee is 'incapacitated' (at least four days off work). There is no entitlement for the employee for the first three days unless they have previously been off sick in the last two weeks. There are other implications, and a leaflet from the DSS is useful to keep on file for all the pertinent details.

Maternity pay and leave

The employee has to have been working for you full-time for a qualifying two-year period. In addition she must tell you whether she will be off work, fully or partly, due to her pregnancy. She is entitled to attend ante-natal clinics, with pay, providing you receive proof of appointment. You can ask for confirmation (written or verbal) of her pregnancy and the time she will need off, and also whether she intends to return to work after the confinement. If she fails to do this, and providing that you have previously let her know that under the circumstances she would not be re-employed, that it is not reasonably practicable to take her back as there is no suitable position. And lastly, if you currently employ less than six people, then she can be fairly dismissed.

Ending employment

You can fire anybody you want for any reason you want. This is your right. However, remember that if it is not done correctly you may be letting yourself in for any one of a number of subsequent problems. Keep to the golden rule: discipline. If you discover something that necessitates action, the first thing you must do is investigate what has happened. The second thing you must do is tell your employee what the complaint is, and why. Then you must listen to his side – and that really does mean listening. Only then do you go to the fourth step and make your decision. Get any one of those four out of order and it is an unfair dismissal. Many people will be delighted to represent the other side. It is as simple as that – get the four stages in the correct order and it can be said that you have behaved reasonably.

The formal procedure demands that there is a stage when you let the employee know that you are taking the issue seriously – the verbal warning. But you need to confirm this in writing because you then have a record on file. This written warning must be followed by a final written warning, again kept on file. There may not be a need for the written warning; you can make do with a final warning in most companies because, as the tribunals have said, in a small company you know when you are fitting in.

The underlying principle behind any disciplinary procedure is to improve performance. It is not there to sack people or punish them but to improve the performance of your business.

The disciplinary decision must be appropriate. Take the story of Joe who was probably the top fitter of a small engineering company, but his time-keeping was appalling. Finally Joe's manager called him in and said, 'If you are not in on time for the next 28 days I am going to fire you.' Joe was on time for 28 days but on the twenty-ninth day was late again. The manager fired him; Joe then went to a tribunal and won. It was judged an unfair dismissal because it was what is known as a 'resolute warning'. What he should have said was: 'Joe, you will be fired if you are late during the next 28 days, and thereafter you will be expected to obey the standards demanded by the firm's rules.' They could then have fired him quite fairly if he misbehaved thereafter.

If you dismiss someone it has to be fair and for a good reason and you must act reasonably in the way you dismiss the person. Let us consider an example of this. You want your secretary to take a letter or answer a telephone in the morning, but she is not there because she is late in. You get increasingly annoyed with this and declare that if your secretary is late once more – after three warnings – you will sack her. Sure enough, she comes in late the following day and you sack her. In isolation, that seems entirely reasonable and a good reason for sacking. But you might find that there are one or two more employees like her who habitually come in late, but because they do not work directly for you their lateness has not been noticed and you have not taken any action against them. Your secretary may know about this and she could complain to an industrial tribunal, that whilst she was late, she was unfairly dismissed because other people were allowed to be late and they were not dismissed.

Among the grounds for dismissal are: capability, conduct, and that catch-all 'any other reasons substantial enough to warrant termination of employment' (remember to look closely at what is included in the contract of employment).

Employers often forget that they can also dismiss people because of their effect on customers. There is the case of the receptionist for a well-known firm of architects. One day she came in with badges all over her chest. One said 'Lesbians Unite' and gave a telephone number, another offered homosexual advice, again with a telephone number, and so on. The senior partner took her aside and said that her personal views could well upset some of the customers who might not share them. The receptionist removed the badges; however, one day she came in with a very large badge which again displayed the same messages. The company fired her and she took them to the tribunal. She lost her case because of the effect that her actions could quite reasonably be thought to have on customers. There are similar grounds for dismissal if an employee's actions affect other employees adversely.

Most employers are too timid to manage. If you have real problems with an employee, go through the reasonable process. In the end if it does not work, then you must be firm as you have the responsibility to the people who remain. Your over-riding responsibility is for the continuance of the company. You must also behave properly at all times. Any manager who, in the formal disciplinary procedure, uses bad language, for instance, has evidently lost control; either that or he has such a limited vocabulary that it is doubtful whether he ought to be a manager at all. You must also be precise in your language and give a very clear indication of what is happening. Remember the contract, operate the proper procedures during employment, and on termination, and do as you would be done by.

Tribunals

The penalties for unfair dismissal can be high. Compensation runs on average at about £600 to £1,000. Very often, even though you might have a good case, you may be tempted to consider settling out of court for what has often been called a 'blackmail sum'. This is not morally a good idea but is good commercially because defending a complaint of unfair dismissal will mean spending a lot of time preparing a case and waiting for it to be heard and possibly, adjourned. In addition, there is the expense involved. But you should bear in mind that paying out makes it look as though your company gives in easily to accusations of unfair dismissal. You might therefore be running the risk of facing further prosecution.

If the employee resigns

Be careful of the person who leaves your employment and who is not dismissed. Somebody may give in their notice and leave, yet that may still be taken to be a dismissal if that person left because of actions by the employer making the employment untenable. To take an extreme example, if you were trying to persuade your chief accountant to falsify the figures, he might well leave your employment. He would then be justified in complaining of an effective dismissal because you were asking him to do something that was outside his contract of employment.

Generally, the test is whether the employer's action could be construed as going to the root of the contract. Always get a letter of resignation, or use a termination form. It is good practice in human relations if somebody is leaving to sit down and say: 'I'm sorry you are leaving – when do you want to go? What are you going to do?' It is also excellent practice in employment terms, because you will in all likelihood be getting at that stage an honest answer. Subsequently, you will be able to point out that you did your best to make sure you understood the reason for leaving and that nobody gave you an opportunity to put any matter right that was later complained of. Employment law once again marches hand in hand with common sense.

Redundancy

There are two aspects to redundancy: human and financial. The human aspect encompasses such points as giving the employee longer than the statutory notice and adequate time off to find another job. The financial side depends on the prevailing market conditions in the industry or the company, and it is not unusual for some companies to pay considerably in excess of statutory terms. Then you should consider items as extra notice, or retention bonuses, if you want the employee to stay on for a period of three months because your order book is going to be full until then. You must decide what you do with employees over 60: do you top up pensions? There are many issues like this which are only solved in the light of experience.

As long as you meet the official redundancy payments, you have carried out the statutory obligations. The first thing to remember is that legislation is meant to help you. If you can show that it is for the continuing good of your business, it will normally be fair for you to declare a redundancy. You must show that you have fairly selected the people who will be made redundant. This can depend on how you have done it before, which would then be taken as customary practice. You can also use the 'last in first out' principle, which is often management's easy way out. Offering early retirement could produce the right number of job terminations for you to meet your redundancy allocation; this action is often the first one to consider.

Getting help

Small employers looking for help should not accept glossy packages backed by insurance. Any policies in your company must be yours and you must have had a part in making them, agreeing them and setting them up; if you do not do this, then you are avoiding a large part of your managerial responsibilities. If you are going to ask for legal advice, do take the sensible steps of enquiring whether the advisers have specialised in employment law and whether they have had any experience in this field. Ask for references, ask whether or not these companies operate in similar business fields. Find out their company size, the number of personnel and their financial turnover. Check this out with the management and consultancy associations, otherwise you invite problems.

Conclusion

Some of the foregoing material, because of the implications, may seem somewhat negative, but do not let it frighten you away. Employment is basically a matter of common sense. From the start, be sure that you follow the proper procedures; if you do this you will avoid many of the hair-raising aspects. Correct procedure and proper communication are vital ingredients, and will be appreciated not only by yourself but also by your employees, as they in turn will know precisely where they stand and who they are dealing with. We have not delved into the matter of effective communication once an employee is working for you, or the managerial aspects necessary for firm and positive personnel practices; they must, nonetheless, be taken into account and put into practice in any situation where it is necessary. The key must be good administration, well-defined procedures and positive communication and management.

10 Starting off in export

There is only one good reason for exporting and that is for profit. It is not the sort of activity to launch yourself into just because you are having a rough time in the UK. It is very hard work and if you make mistakes in overseas markets they can be even more expensive than the mistakes you may make at home. The first question you need to ask is, 'Do I need to go into the export market at all?' If your company has excess capacity and you find that your market at home is static, there are many other possibilities, of which exporting is but one. The only time you should get involved in selling outside your home market is when you have gone into the matter thoroughly and satisfied yourself that it is going to be a commercially sensible means of generating some profit.

But what if you have got a good product which could be exported? First, you must stand back and take a long, hard look at your company, and ask yourself a few more questions, such as whether your product will sell in an overseas market. Take a closer look at the available market in the country of import, and decide whether or not you can adapt if required. Should your export drive be successful, can you cope with the increased production demand? And what about additional capital? Do you have the necessary skills in shipping and can you speak the language of the country you are dealing with?

Answering these questions honestly will go a long way in helping you to make a decision as to whether or not you should consider going into the export market. But before you go any further you should go along to either the head office or the regional head office of your bank and discuss your project with the international division. They will be able to tell you about the currency and legal restrictions of the particular country which you anticipate exporting to; they can help in the preparation of credit documents, and much more.

The one thing you can be sure about is that it is going to cost money. First, you will have to spend time and effort on research to get the right information about the potential market place. Secondly, if you do decide to export, you can be certain that you will spend more than you will gain for the first few years. Companies who have been successful in the export market were prepared to get into the market and stay there, knowing that eventually the business would work. British management tends not to like doing that. In this country we work to one-year budgets, while the Japanese, for instance, are prepared to spend the money knowing that they will succeed and work to budgets of longer duration. You have to be prepared for it to take at least two or three years to see a market grow, and that means you have to be careful not to invest more than you can afford. But it is not only money that is important; motivation also plays a key role. Ask yourself: 'Is my company actually committed to the export business? Is there someone in my organisation who is prepared to monitor the work and make sure that it is properly followed through?'

What can we export? There are three possibilities: products, services and know-how. The easy way of doing things is licensing the 'know-how'. You do not have to get involved in shipping goods and therefore it costs less, but the difficulty is to make sure that the legal details are absolutely correct. If you are considering products, you need to be sure that your production can cope, that your finances are good, that the sales contract is established and running smoothly and, of course, that you have the right staff. A good shipping manager, or consultant, can save you a great deal of time and money.

The next question should be, 'Which country should I export to?' There is no easy answer. English is the main commercial language of many countries, but if that is not the case with the country you want to export to, then it is essential to speak your customer's language. If you cannot speak the language yourself or employ a bilingual assistant, there are translation services available not only from the Chambers of Commerce but also offered by privately owned companies.

Selling overseas is an attractive proposition. It is a way of spreading your risks in different economies; however, do not forget that if the home economy is not doing too well, the foreign one may also have problems. Bear in mind too that the importing country may not consider your product in the same light as you do, and that you will have competition, not necessarily from this country, but probably from Japan, West Germany and Holland.

Researching your market

In order to be successful you have to understand what overseas customers want, and there are only two ways to find out: doing some basic desk research, and going out to ask them. Let us assume that you are going to start doing business in Holland. Go to one of the major exhibitions related to your industry and look around; it will give you the chance to find out not only how your potential customers see you and your product, but also discover your own attitude towards them. Talk to people and find out how your product could fit into their market.

Investigate the cost of shipping, including packaging and freight, import duties and sales taxes which will be levied on your product. Within the EEC there are no tariff barriers but you have to remember that VAT is levied at different rates in different countries.

Then there is marketing and sales support to

consider. Ask yourself, 'Do I have the financial resources to keep this going, especially if the going gets tough?' You also need to be sure that your product is the right quality for the market. This may not mean that it has to be of a very high quality, just that it has to be of the level of quality for which the customer in that particular country is willing to pay. It is usually better to look for the higher price and to go up-market. Why? Because you can be certain that it is going to cost you more to get into the overseas market than you had imagined. Therefore if you can aim your product at the premium price sector, you are more likely to be able to pay for your efforts and make a profit. The other consideration is that in many of the European markets as well as in the USA, Australia and New Zealand, people are more willing to pay a higher price if they recognise the product as being good value. Many overseas markets are not as price-conscious as the UK, but design, packaging and promotion are all important.

Your market strategy

The key to successful market entry can be considered under three headings: analysis, assessment and action.

First, analysis. Consider all the known facts and establish your reason for seeking entry to that particular market. Examine the operation in your existing markets. Find out why your products are bought and sold. This may sound obvious, but there was one company in the West Midlands, with a splendid sales record to an African state who finally discovered that it was the packaging that was in demand rather than the product. It might have been better if, in those circumstances, they had exported their packaging only!

Are your sales in existing markets due to longstanding personal relationships? If so, avoid complacency – these markets might be at risk when the present managing director retires. What is the competition like both at home and abroad? Know your share of the market. Self-examination is the first step and does not cost you anything but your time. It is also important at this stage to encourage a whole-hearted commitment within the company towards developing the new market.

Secondly, assessment. It is obviously better to saturate one market than to try to become a worldwide exporter overnight by exporting to 27 different countries. If you are a newcomer to exporting, start off near home in a market which is big enough for you to be able to get reasonable sales. Markets are collections of particular people who want to buy your kind of product, so it is not total numbers that matter. There are many countries in the world with large populations but they do not necessarily have any interest in your kind of product, or the income to buy it. Look for a market which has some growth potential.

Ideally, you want a market that is stable. For example, underdeveloped countries dependent on oil for their revenue might stop importing if the oil price plummets. Many people spent a lot of money developing business in Iran, only to see it collapse overnight. There is little you can do to prevent that happening but you should be aware of the dangers.

One of the disadvantages of selling abroad is the language problem, therefore a number of people prefer selling to the Australians or the Americans. Although we may think that we speak the same language as the Americans, very often we do not understand each other. It costs a lot of money to develop, monitor and seek out new business in America and success stories such as Jaguar Cars do not happen very often. So first consider your market-place in Europe. You could start perhaps in Holland, and establish business with people who have a good command of the English language, have 'English' tastes and very similar industries. Then, once established, you could consider expanding into the rest of Benelux. You will find that once your product is successful there it would, with very little alteration, sell quite successfully in West Germany – a huge market which is bigger than the UK and a lot richer. With some amendments to packaging and presentation you could also sell in France and Scandinavia.

Look at countries with traditional UK trading connections. It would probably be wise to avoid countries which are unstable either politically or economically (or both); a country such as Lebanon would currently come into this category.

Beware of countries who are noted for being poor payers because of the lack of foreign exchange; your bank will tell you which ones these are. Remember that in such countries the importer will often pay in local currency upon demand, but payment in foreign exchange will be deferred, pending an allocation being made available by the central bank, and this can result in long delays. For instance, your buyer in Zambia may well pay for the goods upon first request but it has been known to take up to 27 months, if not longer, for foreign exchange to be made available by the central banks in Zambia to send back to the UK. This is obviously not good for your business, so in such cases you should look for a more secure method of settlement such as a documentary letter of credit.

Look closely at the oil-rich countries and those with oil that are still in the process of developing this important natural resource. Look also at the ease of access to, and communications with, those countries. In many countries the telephone system and postal services leave a lot to be desired. To export into one country often involves going through some other country's port; you must look carefully at the political and economic futures of both countries, and at the cost of transport. The further away the market, the greater the cost to get your product there. It will also be more difficult to make regular service visits to your clients, and these, after all, are the essence of good business relations. You would not dream of selling to customers in this country whom you did not regularly visit and talk to, and it is no different if you are selling overseas. Indeed, it is even more important to visit your overseas customers regularly because they know less about you, are less aware of your product, and, even though you may have been in business for a century, they have not had the experience of dealing with your company.

Consider what kind of distribution network you want to set up, and the timing of it. You may be fortunate enough to find either a distributor or a local representative in the country to which you are exporting. Do not decide that you want distributors in 10 different countries and appoint them all at once. You will find that they soon become disillusioned because, 'We never see anybody from your company, nobody ever has the time to come here.' You have to get to know them just as you do your UK customers, and work closely with them.

Are you going to sell directly to someone who will buy and use your product or are you going to sell to somebody who in turn distributes to other customers? Are you going to sell to another manufacturer who has a sales force, and want to incorporate your product into his range? It may be that he will want you to take one of his products and sell it in the UK – a back-to-back operation – and that can work very well. The danger is that almost inevitably you either export more or import more, but you very rarely get a balance. As long as you recognise the pitfalls, that is one way of doing good business. It is essential, of course, to examine what kind of profitability you expect and how much in terms of resources you can allocate.

By now you have made your assumptions and picked out your target markets, but it is still not necessary to commit the company to any great expenditure other than your own time. There are many sources of free information which enable you to proceed to the third step – action. As in any business, the most important thing is to set yourself objectives. It does not matter if you write them on the back of an envelope or whether you have a super marketing plan, as long as you have a clear and realistic set of goals. In other words, do not imagine that you are going to move in and steal 10 per cent or even 30 per cent of someone else's market overnight. You cannot do it in the UK, and you cannot expect to do it overseas. In fact, there are advantages in going in fairly quietly and getting to know and understand the market. By the time people are aware of your presence, it is too late for them to do anything about it. The last thing you want to do is to sound the trumpets and go in with a lot of noise, because your competitors will do their best to see that you are not successful.

Pricing your product

Exporting can place a great burden on cash flow and can cause financial headaches, therefore it is very important that everybody in the organisation, whether the production manager, or the marketing manager, or the sales manager, understands the concept of profitability. Different companies quite sensibly look at profits in different ways: a return on investment or a return on assets employed. Define it how you will, but make sure that everybody in the business is measuring their profitability in exactly the same way. The salesman who goes abroad must know how the costs are built up and what element of contribution or profit there is. Then he is in a position to negotiate.

On the assumption that you are going to invest money for a period of time, you have to ensure that the price at which you sell is going to allow you to make the effort. It is far better to set a higher price and give extra service and proper support for a good product than to sell too cheaply. The important thing is to establish the true cost of doing business in the country. Remember that when you are getting into selling abroad one of the most crucial factors, just as in the UK, is establishing the right price. It is very easy to go in at too low a price. If you are in any doubt then always move up-market and not down-market. It is always easy to come down but it is very difficult to go up. Make sure you build into your prices all the expenses you will incur such as travelling overseas, sending out samples, having brochures produced and printed in languages other than English, spending time with distributors, having visits from your overseas contacts whom you will have to entertain and look after. Allow too for a number of false starts when you do not quite get things right, the costs of developing your product further, the changes in packaging and labelling. On this point, do not forget that there are companies overseas – for example, another manufacturer or a retail group – who may be very willing to share the cost with you.

Look at your product from the customer's point of view, and at the price. The customers are buying benefits. What your customer is concerned about is what it will do for him and what it will cost. So when you are positioning your product and its price, think of all the benefits you are building in. For example, if you are selling on credit, that is a benefit and it has to be paid for and included in the price. If you are providing technical support, that is a benefit – make sure the customer knows about it. If you are providing a lot of brochures, or offering training for your customer's staff to come back to this country in order to visit the factory, those are benefits which can be highlighted in your pricing structure.

The further away your customer is, the more links there are in the distribution chain, and the more problems there are created every time you increase the price. If you put 5 per cent on your price in this country and then ship it in and the customer has to pay the import duty, he pays the import duty on the original price plus 5 per cent. He then has to take his margin as well as give a discount to a retail organisation or another distributor, and so the price builds up. What customers overseas want is not necessarily low prices but, as far as possible, stable prices. With currency fluctuations, you lose that stability. UK producers' prices go down when sterling weakens, but customers overseas do not necessarily reduce their prices. Their customers say, 'I've gained 5 per cent, and anyway the price will go up again before long.' In some European countries inflation has been running at a lower rate than in the UK, so if you say to your West German buyer that you have got to increase your price by 10 per cent, or even 15 per cent to keep in line with inflation, it does not go down very well, understandably. He says, 'We managed with 5 per cent inflation; I cannot import your 10 per cent extra inflation into my country.' When you are putting your package together you must therefore establish a price with a view to being able to maintain it for a reasonable period of time. If you think that it will have to go up in six months' time, it is better to go into the market at that price from the outset rather than to come into it cheaply.

In the UK we tend to be less flexible in our export pricing. Prices are cost-based; you look at what it cost you to make the product and what it will cost you to ship it. They bear no relation to what you might ask for the product in the market concerned. It is much more important to structure your price to appeal to the particular customer. You may find that you can command a very much higher price. Alternatively, you may find that you are just not going to be competitive, and then you have either got to accept a lower price – with all its consequences – or not go into the market at all.

Using your own sales force

The easiest entrance to some export markets may be through well-established export merchants' houses and the confirming houses. These people have been in the export business since the days of sailing ships; you will find them in the trade directories. There are a number of advantages in using a merchant as a medium. He will take care of the financial risk, pay you more or less from the point of dispatch of your goods, handle the documentation (some of it is quite complex and certainly time-consuming; any time you spend on documentation is money and it comes out of your pocket), and receive enquiries from all parts of the world. Once you have made a contact with an exporter or a confirming house for one market he will constantly be feeding you with possibilities for other markets.

The alternative is your own sales force (plus agents or distributors). Choose them carefully. Overseas buyers often say that some British salesmen come in with notebooks in which they write the questions asked of them and then depart, saying, 'Thank you very much for your time, I will now go directly back to my sales director and ask whether we can meet your requirements. We will be writing back to you.' Unfortunately, many of them do not go straight back to their companies because they are on a three-week tour. When they finally return they cannot always follow everything that they have written down in their notebooks.

You should have salesmen abroad who can make decisions, who have discussed the possibilities for alterations if need be, know how costs are arrived at and how flexible pricing is, and what they can do to make it easier to get the business. Any information they still lack can be supplemented by telephone or telex. When each salesman returns he must follow up all the things he was going to do. He should write a report of the visit and put in the margin the name of the person who is to deal with the request. This must be circulated and a meeting held with those concerned.

Good communications are essential. If you come back from seeing somebody abroad, write them a letter. If you are lucky they will reply to it, but English may not be their language. Your letter may also be mistranslated, or the reply you receive may seem brusque. This is because of the language barrier. Many of us just pick up the telephone. When you speak to someone on the telephone you can find out immediately whether you have been understood. Do not assume though that, because your client speaks excellent English, he actually reads and understands it to the same degree. In Scandinavia you find that most people have a very good command of spoken English, as do the Dutch, Belgians and Germans; the French and Italians too have a good command of the language, albeit to a lesser extent. Generally, in Europe, English is understood and used as a commercial language. Ask questions of your overseas customers and be sure that they mean what you mean; it is all too easy for misunderstandings to arise, no matter how good their command of English appears to be. The advantage of being able to speak your customer's own language cannot be exaggerated; you have only to think how a Frenchman who speaks no English would sell in Birmingham. There are, however, many countries in the world where you can manage quite successfully.

A lot depends on your product. If you are selling a highly technical product and have to explain it to the man who is going to use it – who may not be a technician, nor even a qualified engineer, but the man on the shop floor – then you cannot reasonably expect him to speak your language. In exporting you often have to become a bit of a diplomat, treading carefully but making absolutely sure that each side knows exactly what the other is talking about.

Getting paid

All too often you hear of someone who has landed some handsome unsolicited order from some faraway exotic country. Delighted in his good fortune he makes the goods and sends them off, usually by air-freight and on open account, then he sits back and waits to get paid. This is the way he normally does business in the UK. So he waits and waits and nothing happens, then he makes enquiries and finds out that his buyer has picked up the goods and disappeared without leaving any arrangements for payment. He has a financial loss on his hands. Increasingly, export orders that come in like this are accompanied by fraudulent guaranteed payment orders or letters of credit. Many of them are very sophisticated and it does take an expert to sort out which ones are trustworthy.

This financial risk could have been avoided had the exporter taken one or two fairly simple precautions.

More important, it would have been better had he anticipated receiving that order and established his company's export strategy well in advance of the event, enlisting the help of specialists outside his own company, many of whom supply their services free.

One of the ways in which you can solve the problem of credit control is by talking to your bank and making sure that you take out adequate references on overseas customers, insisting – if you like – on trading on the basis of an irrevocable letter of credit which is payable on a London bank. This method is the safest as it guarantees payment, but unfortunately it inhibits a lot of people from doing business with you. Every time you protect yourself you make it more difficult for people to do business with you, and you will have to make a decision on how to strike an equal balance. In risky markets it is always better to play safe and work on the basis of a letter of credit. When you start to develop a small business talk to the Export Credits Guarantee Department; you can then insure 90 to 95 per cent of the risk, provided, of course, that you take the normal, elementary precautions.

Where to go for information

The British Overseas Trade Board

There are many organisations whose job it is to help you succeed in exports. The DTI has assumed the role previously occupied by the British Overseas Trade Board, and must be first on the list. It provides information, advice and help by directing the gathering, storing and dissemination of overseas market information, and by stimulating export promotion publicity. Its related services include a market intelligence library in London for statistical research, where you will also find a wide selection of important information and reference books, ranging from the Who's Who for Los Angeles to the telephone directories for Helsinki. It is well worth someone from your company who is proficient in the relevant language spending a day going over your particular target market and finding contacts that might be useful.

There are several DTI offices covering the UK, and contact with your nearest branch would be advisable. Detailed booklets are available from, for instance, its special division on projects and export (PEP) and its export documentation section (SITPRO). Full details are to be found in Appendix IV. SITPRO are able to provide very useful documentation master copies, and if you are preparing all documentation yourself, then these forms will be of great assistance.

The DTI also has an export market research scheme which employs professional market researchers to advise exporters on the best methods of research in markets outside Europe. In approved cases the DTI will make substantial contributions towards the cost of such research. If you have a market research department, they may well be prepared to pay up to one half of the cost of the staff on a specific project. Research conducted through a chamber of commerce or trade association can get two-thirds of the cost covered by the DTI. They can help with documentation and also supply some of the more obscure documents which you are going to require under letters of credit.

The Export Intelligence Service

The EIS is a computerised information service provided by the DTI which distributes export intelligence daily to subscribers. It has a computer which receives input from various consulates and attachés abroad, detailing export opportunities for UK suppliers. You tell the computer what you want and it gives you the information tailor-made.

The Chamber of Commerce

Other major providers of export expertise are the Chambers of Industry and Commerce. The two largest are probably the London and Birmingham chambers, both of which have libraries where further research can be carried out. The Birmingham Chamber information desk handles some 140,000 enquiries each year. The chambers organise and lead overseas trade missions in conjunction with the DTI, for which generous financial assistance towards the cost is often available. They also become involved in joint ventures sponsoring exhibitors at selected industrial exhibitions.

The Institute of Export

The function of the Institute, which was formed in 1935, is 'To set and raise the standards of export practice and management through training, formal and informal education and the exchange of ideas and information between exporters.' It runs two-year courses in export practice with a diploma upon successful completion.

With a wide range of companies and individuals as members (approximately 5,000) the Institute of Export is able not only to give advice and assistance but also to introduce to each other fellow exporters who have areas of mutual interest. As it has established branches in all the major centres in the UK, the Institute is an extremely useful organisation for all exporters.

Other sources of help and advice

The commercial attachés to the various British embassies and consulates abroad are very helpful. They do a lot of work on behalf of the export business. If you do travel overseas, a visit to the commercial attaché or consulate is a must, even if it is just to introduce yourself, as they keep up to date with the markets. In addition, there are a number of specialist trade associations keen to expand their members' interests abroad; you should see if your own association will help.

Before you rush off to your local cut-price travel office to book your ticket for your overseas trip, visit a business travel expert. If you tell him exactly what you want to do and where you want to go, he will put together an itinerary which may save you several hundred pounds. It is well worth spending a little time and trouble with travel agents when you are deciding to go abroad.

The banks

The services offered to exporters by the international divisions of the major banks fall broadly into two categories. First, those services which will assist you in marketing your product; secondly, those services which offer assistance once a sale is proceeding (for instance, the various types of documentation and the various methods of settlement that can be employed, and the various forms of finance available to exporters). Find out from your local branch the address of their regional head office or the location of their international division.

A good starting point is the economic reports which all the large banks provide. They contain information on the political and economic conditions of all major countries and are produced by their own marketing intelligence departments. The National Westminster Bank, for instance, publishes economic reports on some 70 countries and these are freely available on request to anyone, customers or non-customers. Banks can also supply additional information on overseas markets, either from their own staff who are operating in those markets or from their executives who have special international responsibilities.

You may consider that the most appropriate way to conduct your business is by opening a branch office or setting up a subsidiary operation abroad. Here again the banks can produce useful guides which cover the types of operation which are allowed by local laws, and give details of such things as labour regulations and local tax systems. Each guide also gives a contact for further information. However, opening an office abroad is not a route to be followed without a great deal of thought; many companies have lived to regret such a decision through not having done sufficient research beforehand.

Once you have chosen one or two likely countries you

would like to sell to, the banks may be able to assist you in locating potential buyers abroad through their trade enquiry service. To take advantage of this scheme, you must give the bank an exact description of the type of goods you have on offer, and some publicity material. A good brochure gets a much better response than an ordinary explanatory letter. If you want to sell in France then at least half of your brochure must be in French. Similarly with West Germany or Belgium, although they are a little more amenable to English language brochures.

The banks need to know what type of contact you are hoping to make, whether it is with an agent, or a direct importer, or a wholesale distributor. With this information the banks will contact their associate or correspondent banks in the countries of your choice. They in turn will endeavour to find a customer on their books who is looking to import those goods. If a suitable customer is found, his name and address are passed back, together with a status report given by the bankers.

At this point the bank will pass this information on to you and withdraw. It is then up to you to take the matter further. Names passed on are usually the names of companies abroad who are definitely looking for a supply of your goods. They are aware of your existence, and they will want to know a little bit more about you. There are usually seven or eight responses for each of the enquiries sent out, and business is generated from these introductions. This service is free, though you may be asked to contribute towards the cost of sending out catalogues if they are heavy. This is an easy and inexpensive way of investigating a new market. If the banks do not produce any names then it may be an indication that the particular country is not the place for your product. Conversely, if a dozen names come up, then it will always be worth taking a trip abroad to visit the contacts and follow them up. When that time comes it could be useful to go armed with a letter of introduction to a bank in the area. The local banker will know his area and could be helpful in putting you in touch with other export opportunities, or he may assist you in obtaining some urgent status information or bankers' opinions, as well as arranging a letter of introduction.

Now that you have achieved some contacts abroad, your salesman can take over. If you are selling to people such as ICI or Philips, you are safe, but generally you are going to be dealing with people you have never heard of before, so status reports from your bank are essential. All banks have a credit information service through which they can obtain reports on the general standing and creditworthiness of overseas buyers and agents. If you can provide details of the company in question, such as the full name and address, trade references, names of directors and, of course, the name and address of the company's bankers, then your UK bank should be able to give you a full report fairly quickly. If the banks need to get further information, they will normally use airmail, but if you are willing to pay the charges then telex or cable can be used.

If you want more information than the normal bank financial report, contact the DTI as they should be able to help. If, for instance, you were considering appointing an agent, it would be quite reasonable to want to know rather more about him than just his financial standing. For a fee, the DTI will undertake its own status report which will look into the agent's success, or lack of it, in his own field, and his reputation in the trade, and assess his suitability to act as an agent for you. You must then see him and make the final decision yourself.

Once you are involved in exporting, it is important to keep abreast of any changes abroad and again the banks can help with their regular bulletins. They also list some of the export opportunities noticed during the preceding months and give news of overseas trade, new international and EEC laws and regulations and so on. Perhaps the most valuable part is that which gives details of the countries where there are problems in obtaining payment. Finally they give details of exporters' seminars. Ask at a local branch to be put on the mailing list for these exporters' bulletins, even if you are not a customer. There is also a useful series of books entitled *Hints to Exporters* issued by the DTI. Each one covers a single country and gives you all the basic information that you need to know, from how to behave in that country, what is accepted and what is not, which are the working days and which are public holidays. There is a wide range of publications in this field and it is worth spending some time finding out which suits your business best.

Smaller Exporters Schemes

Because of the speed in exporting goods to the Continent and in order to minimise the exporter's problems in administering his own ECGD Comprehensive Insurance Policy, as well as to provide easier export finance, some banks have introduced a 'Smaller Exporters Scheme'. These vary in detail, but the basic principle is that the bank is the ECGD policyholder and handles the paperwork, giving cover against the usual risks. Fixed rate post-shipment finance can be arranged in approved cases on presentation of shipping documents to the bank. These schemes involve rather more expense for the exporter than administering his own ECGD policy and taking advantage of the preferential finance associated with an ECGD Bankers' Guarantee, but nevertheless, where management time is of prime importance this method should be considered.

Invoicing in foreign currencies: the exchange rate

Foreign exchange is one of the wilder beasts in the export jungle and you have to be extremely careful not to get the wrong side of it. A new exporter would be well advised to invoice in sterling, at least initially, but this can, and often does, meet with the disapproval of your foreign buyer. If you do have to bow to the wishes of your overseas client and invoice in his currency in order to secure the contract, then this will involve you in a degree of risk called Foreign Exchange Exposure. This means that, while you know the rate of exchange on the day you tender for the contract (the 'spot' rate), you will have no way of knowing the exact rate of exchange on the day you receive payment on the sale. In order to minimise this risk you have three options: a foreign currency account, a forward exchange contract or foreign currency borrowing.

Foreign currency accounts

If you have income and expenditure in the same currency, then a bank account in that foreign currency can eliminate the risk by matching your currency receivable against your expenditure. However, you would be very lucky to be able to match these exactly and so you should also consider some other method of minimising the risk.

The forward exchange contract

This is by far the most usual method of minimising risk, and is available through all the clearing banks. You can arrange a contract to sell the currency you receive to the bank for delivery at some future date. The rate of exchange is agreed at the time the contract is placed, and is guaranteed no matter what happens to either currency. Contracts may be agreed for maturity at a pre-determined date – a fixed contract – or more usually, as you cannot be sure of the precise day on which the funds will be received, between two fixed dates. This is known as an option contract, and proceeds can be applied against the contract at any time during the options period. The option does not extend to whether or not you complete the transaction, it applies only to when the delivery will take place, and there are penalties if the contract has not been used by the time it matures. It is most important that you establish early contact with your bank if you wish to crystallise your exchange risk in this way. A word of caution however, before you enter into any currency commitments: do check that a market exists for the currency, the amount and the period in question.

Foreign currency borrowing

The third method is less usual but well worth considering if you are invoicing in a strong currency such as the Swiss franc. If you are able to quantify your currency income over a period of six months, then you could borrow that same amount from your bank and exchange it all for sterling on the same day, at the rate of exchange ruling on that day (the 'spot' rate). The sterling equivalent could then be used to reduce your sterling overdraft, or be applied as working capital. In this way you have crystallised your exchange risk right at the outset because when the currency proceeds are eventually received, they will be applied to reduce your currency borrowing. Strong currencies are usually associated with low interest rates, so the bonus here is that your bank will charge interest based on the currency you have borrowed, rather than that applicable to sterling borrowings. If you are fortunate enough to be invoicing in say Swiss francs, then there could be a real saving, and instead of just minimising the exchange risk, you have actually maximised the profits on the currency transaction. Again, it is important that you discuss this with your banker at an early stage, and you must have foreign currency income from your export receivables to repay the borrowing, otherwise you will achieve what you set out to avoid, a loss through foreign exchange exposure.

Exchange rate and currency changes

We have an enormous advantage in the UK in that we are able to use the City of London for currency negotiations. We can buy forward dollars, Swiss francs, Deutschmarks, etc., on the foreign exchange market and so cut out some of the risks. Some 26 currencies are traded every day on the London Exchange. It may be easier for a customer to be invoiced in, say, Dutch guilders, to compare other prices in Holland and to know how much he will have to pay. That does not mean going into every currency and offering your customer the opportunity of buying from you in the currency of his choice, but simply selecting two or three currencies which are generally accepted throughout the world. But bear in mind the disadvantages for a first-time exporter.

If you are invoicing in US dollars and selling to Australia, you will have to consider not just what is happening between the pound sterling and the US dollar, but also what is happening to the Australian dollar in relation to the US dollar. So it does become more complicated. This is another reason for a new exporter to limit the number of countries he is selling to.

Single Administrative Document

As of 1 January 1988 a new system of forms was introduced in all EEC member states. This form was brought out in order to simplify trading between member EEC countries and to produce a computerised communication of customs data. This new form is called the Single Administrative Document (SAD). There are nine forms to choose from depending on what you are exporting and where you are exporting to. Assistance in selecting the correct form for your exporting needs can be obtained from your local Chamber of Commerce.

The form once completed must be signed by a person authorised by your firm as all the facts committed to this document must be correct. Any information found to be incorrect has to be amended and drawn to HM Customs and Excise attention. This form may also be used for importing or in transit goods moving within the Community. Also, there are certain instances where the form can also be used between non-community countries.

Copies of the SAD form can be obtained from HM Customs and Excise. If you wish to print your own form, it must conform to the official specimen and approval must be granted by Customs and Excise. For details on how to obtain the necessary approval contact the Print Procurement Unit, GASD Branch 2A, HM Customs and Excise, King's Beam House, Mark Lane, London EC3R 7HE.

A book is available from HM Customs and Excise entitled *Single Administrative Document Customs Freight Procedures from 1 January 1988*.

Conclusion

The important factors in exporting are not really very different from what is important when you are dealing in the domestic market. You have got to know and understand the business; you have to learn to understand your customers, and the way they work. Bear in mind that you must consider not only your customer's buyer, but also the other people in his organisation. Look at the competition, not only other exports from this country, but also locally manufactured products and imports from other countries.

Knowing the available sources of information, from the banks and the Department of Trade and Industry to the Institute of Export, is vitally important. A pilot scheme is currently being run jointly by the Training Agency and the West Midlands Regional Management Centre in Stoke-on-Trent. This scheme is specifically designed to help small businesses increase their profits through exports. The aim is so select 12 redundant managers, who have had many years of relevant experience and to assign them to businesses who are developing their export market. The Small Firms Service can also help.

Knowing where to find assistance does not only mean turning to government organisations. Freight forwarders are extremely helpful to small exporters, but do approach those who have specific knowledge not only of the geographical area to which you are exporting, but also of your product's market.

Another quality needed in exporting is flexibility.

This is, after all, what marketing and sales is all about. It is identifying what customers either need or can be persuaded to think they need, and then organising the resources of your business to meet those needs, at a profit.

Be aware that your evaluation of your export potential will raise many questions specifically relating to your business, so when making any enquiries do be precise about what information is required. Utilise the various trade associations who are either dedicated to export marketing or who have an export section.

Lastly, remember that exporting is a tough business, but on the other hand it is rewarding not only from the point of view of job awareness but also financially. Above all, you must decide whether you are seriously committed to making your exporting venture a success, and whether your resources – financial, production, manpower – are able to cope.

Appendices

Appendix I: Action checklist

What you should have already checked

- ☐ Is your health, training, enthusiasm adequate? Have your family and friends agreed to compensate for your weaknesses?
- ☐ Have you arranged for the services of bankers, accountants, solicitors?
- ☐ Have you drawn up a profit-and-loss type budget?
- ☐ Have you drawn up a cash flow plan?
- ☐ Have you a business plan set out in writing?
- ☐ Is your potential profit worth all your effort?
- ☐ Is it possible to test the market further before final commitment?
- ☐ Have you checked on sources, quantities, costs, and reliability of material and stock supply?
- ☐ Is your budgeted profitability realistic?
- ☐ Have you registered as a sole trader/partnership or formed a company?
- ☐ Have you had business stationery printed to facilitate purchasing, negotiation, etc., and did you receive a number of different quotes for its printing?
- ☐ What minimum accommodation will you need?
- ☐ Have you prepared a sketch of your layout plan?
- ☐ Have you arranged enough capital?
- ☐ Have you any further reserves (property, cars, or other items?)

If you buy an existing business

- ☐ What will you pay for goodwill, fittings, plant, etc?
- ☐ How will you check that stock, debtors, tax debts, redundancy payments etc., are as claimed?
- ☐ Will you insist upon seeing at least three years' audited accounts?

Factors related to premises

- ☐ Do you know how much space will suffice for, say, three years?
- ☐ Will you commission an estate agent to help you locate premises for purchase or rental?
- ☐ Does a building to your requirements exist or will alterations need to be made?
- ☐ Have you allowed for good access, adequate height, easy loading, sound ventilation, drainage, etc?
- ☐ Who must you contact about alterations to buildings?
- ☐ Have you sought consent or advice on planning, licensing, health, trade, etc?
- ☐ Have you obtained full and thorough plant and equipment installation details?
- ☐ Have you considered the extent of open, secure or bonded storage?
- ☐ Will you require any special services (three-phase or high-voltage electricity, gas, air, etc.)?
- ☐ Are covenants within a lease likely to prove restrictive?
- ☐ What else should be considered in your case?

Factors related to purchasing

- ☐ Do you know how much stock to buy, when to buy it and at what cost?
- ☐ What will unsold stock cost you?
- ☐ Can you store your purchases securely?
- ☐ Have you prepared a stock control system?
- ☐ Have you sought several quotations for supply (in writing)?
- ☐ Have you planned to keep all expenditure to a sensible minimum?
- ☐ Have you arranged insurances?
- ☐ What else should be considered in your case?

Factors related to administration

- ☐ Have you set up your bookkeeping system?
- ☐ Have you considered and set up a credit control system?
- ☐ What other business controls have you set up?
- ☐ Are you aware of tax, including VAT, and National Insurance requirements?
- ☐ Are you aware of the health, welfare and safety regulations?
- ☐ What special paperwork is necessary?
- ☐ What records and filing must be arranged?
- ☐ Will you require telephone and telex services?
- ☐ What else should be considered in your case?

Factors related to marketing

- ☐ Have you a marketing plan?
- ☐ Have you costed your publicity effort?
- ☐ What should your publicity achieve?
- ☐ Will you provide transport?
- ☐ What packaging and delivery policy will you have?
- ☐ Have you prepared your pricing policy to meet the market opportunity?
- ☐ Will you avoid undercutting your experienced and established competitors' prices?
- ☐ Are your quality, service, price adequate?
- ☐ Have you any unique feature about your offer?
- ☐ Are you better, cheaper, quicker, or all of these, than your experienced competitors?
- ☐ Will you do your own selling?
- ☐ Will you offer salesmen commission (on profit or turnover)?
- ☐ What will your selling effort cost?
- ☐ What else should be considered in your case?

Factors related to staffing

- ☐ Have you analysed the jobs which you will offer?
- ☐ Is there an adequate labour force available?
- ☐ Have you contacted the Job Centre concerning staffing regulations?
- ☐ Will you offer training? If so, have you a training plan?
- ☐ Have you prepared or purchased specimen contracts of employment?
- ☐ What pay, holidays, sickness leave, hours of service, etc., will you allow?
- ☐ Have you considered staff rest and hygiene facilities?
- ☐ What else should be considered in your case?

(Reproduced by kind permission of the Department of Employment from the Small Firms Service booklet *Running Your Own Business*.)

Appendix II: The costs of different methods of raising finance

Type of finance	Size of facility	Annual cost
Proprietor's own resources	n/a	Amount of investment income forgone
Private investors	Maximum amount eligible for relief under BES is £40,000 per investor per annum (Fiscal year 1989/90)	Individuals will expect to receive a reasonable return on their investment
Venture capital, in the form of a combination of loan facilities and a minority shareholding	A number of sources provide finance over £200,000 in this form. Sources are more scarce for much smaller amounts. Also several funds operate under the rules of the BES	Dividends and interest may be artificially low at the outset, but investors will be looking for future strong dividend growth and/or good capital returns. Directors' fees, where the investors require board representation
Venture loans, business start loans and other similar loan schemes	Generally these are available for amounts between £5,000 and £15,000; as part of a package. Usually repayable in five years	Banks' base rate plus 3 per cent to 5 per cent, depending on level of risk involved
Government and local authority discretionary assistance under the Industry Act 1972, and the Inner Urban Areas Act 1973	Central government assistance depends on the location and creation of employment. £5,000 per job created is a useful guideline; larger amounts available in special cases	Nil
Specialist financial packages for management buyouts	Between £100,000 and several millions. Loan finance or redeemable pref-shares generally redeemable within ten years	Loans, between 2 per cent and 5 per cent over banks' base rates. Equity investors may require a reasonable dividend yield
Trade credit	Depends on the values of purchases and trade creditors	Difference between discounts lost and interest 'saved'. Loss of supplier goodwill may constitute a 'hidden cost'

Other associated costs	Timescale for applications	Terms and conditions
n/a	n/a	n/a
There may be some legal and professional fees associated with setting up the investment	n/a	The company must be a 'qualifying company' to enable shareholders to claim relief; essentially this means a genuine business venture, not something just set up for tax reasons
Legal costs associated with setting up the venture capital agreement; as a 'rule of thumb' these are between 1 per cent and 2 per cent of the amount raised	This varies, depending on the extent of appraisal required. Investments rarely take less than a month or more than six months to arrange, two–three months being average	An agreement is usually made between the investors and the participators encapsulating the terms of the investment, namely that the participants will use the funds for the purpose envisaged, not start up any other business or change it dramatically and will devote the whole of their efforts to the company. Levels of dividends and directors' remuneration may be specified in the agreement. Rights of separate classes of shares will be set out in the Articles of Association
An arrangement fee may be charged at the outset	Usually between three and six weeks	The lender may request a right to subscribe for a minority shareholding. Participants may be asked to guarantee the loan. Repayment terms will be specified in the loan agreement
Invariably, professional costs will be incurred in making the application	These may vary between one and four or five months, depending on circumstances	Conditions vary with the type of grant. The basic aim is to ensure that funds are used for the stated purpose. The employment created by the project will usually be monitored
Professional fees associated with structuring the deal may be many thousands. Arrangement fees for loans (usually ½ per cent)	Depending on the size and complexity of the deal, this may take between two weeks and three or four months	An agreement will usually be drawn up between the participators and the financing institutions. This will be similar to that for a 'venture capital' investment
None, although extra bought ledger administrative costs may be incurred	Effectively one or two months if payment to suppliers are to be delayed	Supplier terms and conditions of trade usually specify payment within 30 days

Type of finance	**Size of facility**	**Annual cost**
Customer discounts	Depends on the value of monthly sales	Costs of discounts given, less interest saved. Note that a $2\frac{1}{2}$ per cent discount per month costs over 30 per cent per year
Bank overdraft and short-term loans	Limits will depend on the size of the company, strength of its balance sheet, security and guarantees available and ability to repay. Should be used for short term borrowing (i.e. under 12 months)	Usually between 2 per cent and 5 per cent above banks' base rates. 'Blue chip' companies may be able to borrow at finer rates
Bills of exchange	Usually over £75,000 in value. Upper limits depend on the financial strength of the company	Discounts charged are equivalent to an interest cost of between $1\frac{1}{2}$ per cent and 4 per cent over the three months inter-bank rate
Acceptance credits	As for bills of exchange from £250,000	Accepting commission $\frac{3}{8}$ per cent to $1\frac{1}{2}$ per cent; $\frac{1}{2}$ per cent under base – top end of scale
Factoring	Up to 80 per cent of the value of agreed debts, i.e. as a 'rule of thumb' this usually totals around 50 per cent of the total value of trade debtors for most companies	Interest on funds advanced at between $2\frac{1}{2}$ per cent and 4 per cent over banks' base rates. Factoring charge of between $\frac{3}{4}$ per cent and $2\frac{1}{2}$ per cent of turnover
Invoice discounting	Up to 75 per cent of the value of agreed debts, usually slightly less than 50 per cent of the total value of trade debtors for most companies	Interest on funds advanced of between 3 per cent and 6 per cent over the banks' base rate. Handling charge of around $\frac{1}{2}$ per cent of the value of invoices discounted
Asset loan schemes from the clearing banks	£5,000 to £500,000 for periods of up to 20 years	$2\frac{1}{2}$ per cent to $4\frac{1}{2}$ per cent above the banks' base rate
Hire purchase and lease purchase	Up to 100 per cent of the value of the asset to be acquired	Between 3 per cent and 6 per cent over the finance house's base rate

Other associated costs	Timescale for application	Terms and conditions
Sales ledger administration may become more complicated and therefore cost more	At least one month, depending on how quickly customers decide to take advantage of discounts	None
Costs of arranging security may be recharged in certain circumstances, but usually no charge is made. A commitment fee may be charged, at the discretion of the local bank manager, depending on the work required to set up the facility. This should be up to around $\frac{1}{2}$ to $1\frac{1}{2}$ per cent	Very often an answer can be given 'on the spot'. In general the timescale will be a matter of days rather than weeks	Usually banks will require a floating charge over the assets of the business
None – set-up costs are usually absorbed in the discount rate	An initial application for discounting facilities may take up to two weeks to be arranged. Thereafter, bills may be discounted on sight	Discount houses will usually set an upper limit for discounting bills – for both parties to the transaction. Payment terms must be adhered to rigidly
Some banks may charge a commitment fee if the facility is set up but not used for some time	As for bills of exchange	Banks will set an upper limit for accepting bills and will require funds to be available for immediate repayment on maturity
Some companies make a charge of $\frac{1}{4}$ per cent of opening debtors on setting up an arrangement, but in general there are no set-up costs	This depends on the number and nature of the company's customers and the amount of investigation required. Usually an agreement can be set up within a month	The factoring agreement is usually subject to between three and twelve months' notice. The factoring company will have no recourse to any of the company's other assets by way of security
Usually there are no set-up costs	As for factoring, this depends on the amount of initial investigation required and the time taken to set up the arrangement will be similar	An agreement is made between the company and the invoice discounting company setting out the terms of invoice discounting. Guarantees or security are not usually sought
For some loans, there may be an arrangement fee of 1 to 2 per cent	Loans can generally be arranged in a few weeks – larger loans may take up to eight weeks to arrange	Some schemes allow for the asset being acquired to form the only security taken. For most smaller companies, however, a charge over the other assets of the company or a guarantee may be required
None	Subject to satisfactory references being obtained, funds can usually be made available within a week	Finance companies usually have the right to reclaim the goods in the event of default (e.g. by the appointment of a receiver), without being accountable to the company for any of the rentals paid up to the date of default (unlike domestic HP)

Type of finance	Size of facility	Annual cost
Leasing and contract hire	Usually 100 per cent of the value of the asset to be acquired although for assets being financed during construction, the funds acquired may exceed the cost of the amount due to interest charges	Between 3 per cent and 6 per cent over the finance house's base rate for leasing facilities provided by the finance companies. The cost of 'big ticket' leasing will be similar to that for medium term loans, i.e. 2 to 4 per cent over the banks' base rates
ECGD-backed loans for exports	100 per cent of invoice value for the 'bills and notes' scheme; 90 per cent of invoice value for trading on open account	Interest $\frac{5}{8}$ per cent over banks' loan rate. ECGD premium fee $\frac{1}{4}$ per cent to $\frac{1}{2}$; ECGD guarantee fee $\frac{1}{3}$ per cent to $\frac{1}{2}$ per cent
Medium-term loans	£250,000 upwards for periods of three to ten years	Between 2 per cent and 4 per cent over the banks' base rate
Development capital	Usually for £250,000 upwards, but no set limits	Investors will look for a reasonable dividend yield and steady dividend growth
Commercial mortgages	Usually up to 75 per cent of the mortgage value of freehold property, for amounts of £50,000 upwards and for up to two years (may also be available on good quality leasehold property)	Between $1\frac{1}{2}$ per cent and $3\frac{1}{2}$ per cent above the banks' base rate, depending on the size of the mortgage and quality of the company
Sale and leaseback	Market value of the property to be sold	Rent on the property sold. This may, initially, be at a concessionary rate but will be charged at full market rates after the first review
Long-term loans	£1 million upwards, for periods in excess of ten years	Investors will require a yield slightly better than that on similar dated gilts

(Reproduced by kind permission of Robson Rhodes.)

Other associated costs	Timescale for application	Terms and conditions
None	For smaller leases (vehicles and smaller items of equipment) the timescale may be a few days. 'Big ticket' leases generally take several weeks to set up	Default on payment leads to termination of the lease. For leasing of larger items of plant and equipment etc., guarantees or security may be required as institutions tend to look on leasing as unsecured medium term lending
In certain cases, collection charges may be passed on to the company	The interest depends upon the amount of investigation of customer which needs to be carried out before the facility can be given. In general, this may take between two and six weeks	Companies are required to insure all their overseas businesses with ECGD and to make a reasonable attempt to recover the debt before resorting to any claims
Arrangement fee – usually no more than ½ per cent. Any cost of investigation, valuation costs and legal costs invoiced to the bank would be passed on to the company, although this would generally be done 'in-house' by the bank at no cost to the company	This may take up to twelve weeks to arrange, depending on the type of security being taken	Loans are usually secured by fixed and floating charges on the company. In addition, the borrower covenants to maintain a prescribed level of interest cover and current assets
Legal and professional costs associated with setting up the investment. Capital duty at 1 per cent on the shares issued	Funds should generally be arranged within two months. If the company has a good track record this timescale may be reduced	An arrangement will be made between the participators and investing institution, similar to that made for venture capital investments. The investors will generally seek board representation
Investigation costs, survey costs and legal costs are generally passed on to the borrower. As a 'rule of thumb' these are likely to be around 2 per cent of the total borrowed. In some cases an arrangement fee of ½ per cent may be charged	Applications generally take between four and six weeks, the limiting factor usually being the time taken by solicitors and surveyors	A mortgage agreement will be prepaid with conditions for foreclosure in the event of default. Where the mortgage is obtained from an insurance company it may be a condition that an insurance policy be taken out with that company
Valuation costs. Legal and professional costs on the sale and tenancy agreement. Possibly Capital Gains Tax on the disposal	Such a transaction will usually be completed within two months	There will be a standard rental agreement for the letting of the property by the company from its new owner
For long-term loans the costs will be as for medium-term loans (see above)	Two to three months should be allowed, longer if the loan is to be syndicated	Debenture holders will have the right to appoint a receiver in the event of default

Appendix III: Select bibliography

This bibliography lists a range of books of interest but it is not intended to be exhaustive. Specialist bodies such as the Small Firms Service provide thorough booklists. Leaflets from government offices provide a further source of information, either from the government department concerned or from HMSO.

Basic Business Management: Guidelines for the Self-Employed and the Smaller Businesses, 2nd edition, M A Peters (Jordans)

Be Your Own Boss: How to Become Self-Employed, John Blundell (National Federation of the Self-Employed)

Be Your Own Boss – Starter Kit, D S Watkins *et al* (The National Extension College). The NEC also publish a book *Be Your Own Boss – Growth Kit*, J Eversley *et al*. Orders direct from NEC, 18 Brooklands Avenue, Cambridge CB2 2HN.

Cashflow and Credit Management, Valerie Hawkes and Ken Slater (The Daily Telegraph)

Code of Practice No. 3, Time Off for Trade Union Duties and Activities (ACAS)

Company Auditing: Concepts and Practices, 2nd edition, T A Lee (Institute of Chartered Accountants in Scotland)

Company Law, 9th edition, M C Oliver (Pitman)

Corporation Tax: A Working Guide for the Small Business, Ian Hills (The Daily Telegraph)

Croner's Reference Book for the Self-Employed and Smaller Businesses and *Croner's Reference Book for Employers* (Croner Publications Ltd.) From: Croner House, London Road, Kingston upon Thames, Surrey KT2 6SR

The Daily Telegraph Guide to Income Tax, R Thornton (Collins)

Employment Law – A Guide. From: Smaller Business Advisory Services Ltd, 34–6 Streetly Lane, Sutton Coldfield B74 4TU

Finance for New Projects in the UK (Peat Marwick McLintock)

Financial Management for the Small Business: The Daily Telegraph Guide, 2nd edition, Colin Barrow (Kogan Page)

Further up the Organisation, R Townsend (Coronet)

A Guide to Franchising, 4th edition, Martin Mendelsohn (Pergamon Press)

Handbook of Industrial Relations Practice, ed. Brian Towers (Kogan Page)

Handbook of Management, ed. Thomas Kempner (Penguin)

How to Choose the Right Business Premises, Keith Jones (The Daily Telegraph)
How to Choose Microcomputers and Software for Your Business, 2nd edition, Paul Beck (The Daily Telegraph)
How to Promote Your Own Business: A Guide to Low Budget Publicity, Jim Dudley (Kogan Page)
How to Set Up a Co-operative Business (Co-operative Development Agency). From: Broadmead House, 21 Panton Street, London SW1Y 4DR. (Other titles on the subject of co-operatives are available from the agency.)
How to Win Profitable Business, Tom Cannon (The Sunday Telegraph)
Individual Rights of Employees: A Guide for Employers, Department of Employment (HMSO)
Industrial Action and the Law, (Job centres)
International Dictionary of Management, 3rd edition, ed. Hano Johannsen and G Terry Page (Kogan Page)
Know Your Business (British Institute of Management). From: BIM, Management House, Cottingham Road, Corby, Northants. NN17 1TT
Looking Ahead: A Guide to Retirement, Fred Kemp and Bernard Buttle (Pitman)
Management of Trade Credit, 3rd edition, T G Hutson and J Butterworth (Gower)
Managing for Results, Peter F Drucker (Pan)
Marketing Your Business, Jeremy Bond and Mike Tintner (The Daily Telegraph)
Money for Business (Bank of England). From: Economics Division, Bank of England, London EC2R 8AH
Occupation: Self-employed, 2nd edition, Rosemary Pettit (Wildwood House)
101 Ways of Saving Tax, 6th edition, Bill Packer (The Daily Telegraph)
PAYE: A Working Guide for the Small Business, Carol Anderson (The Daily Telegraph)
Penguin Dictionary of Commerce, Michael Green (Penguin)
The Daily Telegraph's Pensions Guide, Barry Stillerman (The Daily Telegraph)
The Pitfalls of Managing a Small Business – and How to Avoid Them, (Dun & Bradstreet)
Rapid Company Growth, John Hazel and Alan Reid (Hutchinson Educational)
Selecting and Managing Personnel, Steve Epps (The Daily Telegraph)

The New Small Business Guide, 3rd edition, Colin Barrow (BBC Publications)
Small Firms Centres Publications, various authors (Small Firms Centres)
Raising Finance: The Guardian Guide for the Small Business, 3rd edition, Clive Woodcock (Kogan Page)
Starting a Small Business, (National Federation of Self-Employed and Small Businesses)
Starting a Business (IR28) and *Employer's Guide to PAYE* (P7) published by the Inland Revenue and available from all local branches
The Story Hayward Business Tax Guide, annual, Mavis Seymour and Stephen Say (Kogan Page)
Successful Marketing for the Small Business: The Daily Telegraph Guide, 2nd edition, Dave Patten (Kogan Page)
Taking Up a Franchise: The Daily Telegraph Guide, 5th edition, Colin Barrow and Godfrey Golzen (Kogan Page)
Tax: A Working Guide for the Self-Employed, Ian Hills (The Daily Telegraph)
The Daily Telegraph's Tax Guide, Leslie Livens (The Daily Telegraph)
Understanding Company Accounts, Bob Rothenberg and John Newman (The Daily Telegraph)
Understanding Company Financial Statements, R H Parker (Penguin Books)
Using the Media, Denis MacShane (Pluto Press)
VAT: A Working Guide for the Small Business, Ian Hills (The Daily Telegraph)
Your Business – the Right Way to Run it, A Elliot (Elliot Right Way Books)

Appendix IV: Useful addresses

Small Firms Service

Operated by the Small Firms Division of the Department of Employment, offering information, sign-posting and counselling. The Service produce a wide range of free booklets on all aspects of running a business. Dial 100 and ask the operator for the national freefone number, 'Enterprise'.

East Midlands
Severn House,
20 Middle Pavement,
Nottingham NG1 7DW
0602 581205

North East
Cale Cross House,
156 Pilgrim Street,
Newcastle upon Tyne NE1 6PZ
091-232 5353

North West
Third Floor, 26–28 Deansgate,
Manchester M3 1RH
061-832 5282

Graeme House,
Derby Square,
Liverpool L2 9HJ
051-236 5756

Scotland
120 Bothwell Street,
Glasgow G2 6NR
041-248 6014

Roseberry House,
Haymarket Terrace,
Edinburgh EH12 5EZ
031-337 9595

Yorkshire and Humberside
1 Park Row,
City Square,
Leeds LS1 5NR
0532 445151

South East
Carlyle House,
Carlyle Road,
Cambridge CB4 3DN
0223 63312

Ebury House,
Ebury Bridge Road,
London SW1W 8QD
01-730 8451

Abbey Hall,
Abbey Square,
Reading RG1 3BE
0734 591733

South West
Sixth Floor,
The Pithay,
Bristol BS1 2NB
0272 294546

Wales
16 St David's House,
Wood Street,
Cardiff CF1 1ER
0222 396116

West Midlands
Ninth Floor,
Alpha Tower,
Suffok Street,
Queensway,
Birmingham B1 1TT
021-643 3344

England

Rural Development Commission

Government agency for co-ordinating the economic and social development of English rural areas. Also provides small factory units and workshops in Special Investment Areas and financial assistance to rural community councils and other bodies. 141 Castle Street, Salisbury, Wilts SP1 3TP (0722 336255) will advise on nearest local organiser

English Tourist Board

Provides a wide range of expert advice on those involved in the tourism and leisure industry. Grants available towards capital costs in the Development Areas (North of England and West Country). Further information from Development Advisory Services Unit, Thames Tower, Blacks Road, Hammersmith, London W6 9EL (01-846 9000)

Wales

Welsh Development Agency

The Small Business Unit offers advisory service, guidance and training on a wide range of business functions and crafts skills. Loans. Head Office: Treforest Industrial Estate, Pontypridd, Mid Glamorgan CF37 5UT (0443 841777)

Local offices:

'Isnant', Glynne Road, Bangor, Gwynedd (0248 370082)
Wrexham Industrial Estate, Wrexham, Clywd (0978 661011)
37 King Street, Carmarthen, Dyfed (0267 235642)
Swansea Industrial Estate, Swansea, W. Glamorgan (0792 561666)

Development Board for Rural Wales

Help for small businesses in mid-Wales. Advisory service; factories and workshops; loans. For information: Marketing Director, Ladywell House, Newton, Powys SY16 1JB (0686 26965)

Wales Tourist Board

Advisory services unit to help new and existing enterprises in the tourist industry. Grants and loans available. Free advisory visits, leaflets and fact sheets. Seminars and farm tourism training courses. Brunel House, 2 Fitzalan Road, Cardiff CF2 1UY (0222 499909)

Scotland

Scottish Development Agency

The Small Business Division offers professional advice and technical instruction to help develop small firms in rural and urban areas. Loans and other capital obtainable; small factories and workshops. Rosebery House, Haymarket Terrace, Edinburgh EH4 3EU (031-337 9595/6)

Highlands and Islands Development Board

Helps finance business ventures through grants, low interest loans and/ or minority shareholdings. Factories and workshops available;

comprehensive advisory and support service. Contact: Director of Industrial Development & Marketing, Bridge House, 27 Bank Street, Inverness IV1 1QR (0463 34171)

Scottish Tourist Board
Tourist industry advisory service gives advice and counselling. Applications for grants and loans considered by Development Division. Free booklets. 23 Ravelston Terrace, Edinburgh EH4 3EU (031-332 2433)

Northern Ireland

Northern Ireland Development Agency
Help for new manufacturing enterprises; guidance on financial incentives offered by Department of Commerce. Can assist with start-up capital and expansion. Maryfield, 100 Belfast Road, Holywood, Co. Down BT18 9QX (02317 4232)

Local Enterprise Development Unit (LEDU)
Promotes indigenous manufacturing and service industries. Advisory service; grants and loans; government factories and sites made available. Special assistance for craftwork. LEDU House, Upper Galwally, Belfast BT8 4TB (0232 491031)

Craft Council

Promotes Britain's artist craftsmen. Offers range of schemes, including workshop training; 'new craftsmen' grants, loans and bursaries. 12 Waterloo Place, London SW1Y 4AU (01-930 4811)

The Design Advisory Service

Part of the Design Council; promotes efficient and novel products. Designer Selection Service introduces customers to suppliers. Offices in regional Design Councils and at 28 Haymarket, London SW1Y 4SU (01-839 8000)

New Town Development Corporation

Contact the Managing Director for information on provision of premises and other assistance for small businesses:

Aycliffe
Basildon
Bracknell
Central Lancashire
Corby
Cumbernauld
Cwmbran
East Kilbride
Glenrothes
Harlow
Irvine
Livingston
Mid-Wales (Newtown)
Milton Keynes
Northampton
Peterborough
Peterlee
Redditch
Runcorn
Skelmersdale
Stevenage
Telford
Warrington
Washington

Co-operatives

Co-operative Development Agency

Represents and promotes the co-operative movement. Advice on how to form, manage and finance a co-operative. Does not provide capital, but can indicate sources of finance and make recommendations. Broadmead House, 21 Panton Street, London W1Y 4DR (01-839 2985)

Industrial Common Ownership Movement (ICOM)

Advice and assistance with setting up worker co-operatives especially legal structures. Consultancy, training and publications. Contact Vassalli House, 20 Central Road, Leeds LS1 6DE (0532 461737)

Action Resource Centre (ARC)

Acts as broker in matching secondees from business and industry to long-term community projects and small enterprises. Help with particular skills given. CAP House, 3rd Floor, 9–12 Long Lane, London EC1A 9HD (01-726 8987)

British Steel Corporation (Industry) Ltd

Offers help and incentives to new industry in areas where BSC modernisation is creating jobs. Incentives in addition to government grants and loans in Special Development and Development areas; in some areas also industrial sites and buildings. BSC (Industry) Ltd., Bridge House, Bridge Street, Sheffield S3 8NS (0472 731612)

Enterprise Zones

Belfast
Clydebank
Corby
Delyn
Dudley
Glanford (Flixborough)
Glasgow, City of
Hartlepool
Inverclyde
Invergordon
Isle of Dogs (London Docklands)
Londonderry
Lower Swansea Valley
Middlesbrough
Milford Haven Waterway
North-East Lancashire
North-West Kent
Rotherham
Salford
Scunthorpe
Speke (Liverpool)
Tayside (Dundee/Arbroath)
Telford
Trafford
Tyneside (Gateshead/Newcastle-upon-Tyne)
Wakefield
Wellingborough
Workington

Central government contact points

England

Corby, Dudley, Telford and Wellingborough
Midlands Enterprise Unit
Department of the Environment
Five Ways Tower,
Frederick Road, Edgbaston
Birmingham B15 1SJ
Telephone: 021-643 8191

Glanford, Rotherham, Scunthorpe and Wakefield
Yorkshire and Humberside Regional Office, Department of the Environment,
City House,
Leeds LS1 4DJ
Telephone: 0532 438232

Hartlepool, Middlesbrough and Tyneside (Newcastle/Gateshead)
Northern Regional Office,
Department of the Environment,
Wellbar House,
Gallowgate,
Newcastle upon Tyne NE1 4TD
Telephone: 091-232 7575

Isle of Dogs
Greater London Planning,
Department of the Environment,
Room C8/06
2 Marsham Street,
London SW1P 3EB
Telephone: 01-212 5385

NE Lancashire
Salford/Trafford,
Speke and Workington
North West Enterprise Unit,
Department of the Environment,
Sunley Building,
Piccadilly Plaza,
Manchester M1 4BE
Telephone: 061-832 9111

NW Kent
South-East Regional Office,
Department of the Environment,
Charles House,
375 Kensington High Street,
London W14 8QH
Telephone 01-605 9016

Scotland

Clydebank, Invergordon and Tayside
Industry Department for Scotland,
New St Andrew's House,
St James Centre,
Edinburgh EH1 3TE
Telephone: 031-556 8400

Wales

Delyn, Lower Swansea Valley and Milford Haven Waterway
Welsh Office,
Cathays Park,
Cardiff CF1 3NQ
Telephone: 0222 824064

Northern Ireland

Belfast
Department of the Environment for Northern Ireland,
Clarendon House,
Adelaide Street,
Belfast BT2 8NR
Telephone: 0232 242486

Londonderry
Department of the Environment for Northern Ireland,
Development Office,
Richmond Chambers,
The Diamond,
Londonderry BT48 6HN
Telephone: 0504 260734

Export

Department of Trade and Industry
For information and advice on exports, contact: Export Services and Promotions Division, 1–19 Victoria Street, London SW1 (01-215 7877). There are regional offices in major cities. In Scotland, Wales and Northern Ireland, the offices are in those of the Department of State.

Institute of Export, Export House, 64 Clifton Street, London EC2A 4HB (01-247 9812)

Institute of Freight Forwarders Ltd., Redfern House, Browells Lane, Feltham, Middlesex TW13 7ET (01-844 2266)

International Chamber of Commerce, Centre Point, 103 New Oxford Street, London WC1A 1QB (01-240 5558)

Simplification of International Trade Procedures Board (SITPRO), Almack House, 26–8 King Street, London SW1Y 6QW (01-930 0532). An independent body set up by the Department of Trade. It has developed a simplification of trade procedures and documents.

West Midlands Regional Management Centre,
Staffordshire Polytechnic, College Road, Stoke-on-Trent ST4 2DE (0782 412143)

Local authorities

Many local authorities – county, district, town and borough councils – can offer help and advice to small firms. Contact the Industrial or Economic Development Officer at County or Town Hall. Information also usually obtainable from local library

Other useful addresses

The Advertising Association, Abford House, 15 Wilton Road, London SW1V 1NJ (01-828 2771)

British Direct Marketing Association, Grosvenor Gardens House, 35 Grosvenor Gardens, London SW1W 0BS (01-630 7322)

British Institute of Management, Small Firms Information Service, Management House, Cottingham Road, Corby, Northants NN17 1TT (0536 204222)

British Insurance Association, Aldermary House, Queen Street, London EC4P 4JD (01-248 4477)

British Safety Council, 62–64 Chancellor's Road, London W6 9RS (01-741 1231)

British Standards Institution, 2 Park Street, London W1A 2BS (01-629 9000)

Companies Registration Office, Crown Way, Maindy, Cardiff CF4 3UZ (0222 388588): for Scotland: 102 George Street, Edinburgh EH2 3DJ (031-225 5774)

Equipment Leasing Association, 18 Upper Grosvenor Street, London W1X 9PB (01-491 2783)

Export Credits Guarantee Department (ECGD) Headquarters: Export House, 50 Ludgate Hill, London EC4M 7AY, details of regional offices available from headquarters (01-382 7000)

Industrial Market Research Association, 11 Bird Street, Lichfield WS13 6PW (05432 263448)

Institute of Administrative Managers, 40 Chatsworth Parade, Petts Wood, Orpington BR5 1RW (0689 75555)

Institute of Chartered Accountants of England & Wales, P O Box 433, Chartered Accountants Hall, Moorgate Place, London EC2P 2NBJ (01-628 7060)

Institute of Chartered Accountants of Scotland, 27 Queen Street, Edinburgh EH2 1LA (031-225 5673)

Institute of Directors 116 Pall Mall, London SW1Y 5ED (01-839 1233)

Institute of Management Consultants, 5th Floor, 32–33 Hatton Garden, London EC1N 8DL (01-242 1803)

Institute of Marketing, Moor Hall, Cookham, Maidenhead, Berks SL6 9QH (06285 24922)

Institute of Personnel Management, IPM House, Camp Road, Wimbledon, London SW19 4UW (01-946 9100)

Institute of Public Relations, Gate House, 1 St John's Square, London EC1M 4DH (01-253 5151)

Investors in Industry (3i), 91 Waterloo Road, London SE1 8XP (01-928 7822)

Law Society, 113 Chancery Lane, London WC2A 1PL (01-242 1222)

Manufacturing Advisory Service (MAS) (Production Engineering Research Association PERA), Melton Mowbray, Leicestershire LE13 0PB (0664 64133)

Marketing Society, Stanton House, 206 Worple Road, London SW20 8PN (01-879 3464)

Market Research Society, 175 Oxford Street, London W1R 1TA (01-439 2585)

National Federation of Self-Employed and Small Businesses Ltd., 32 St Anne's Road West, Lytham St Annes FY8 1NY (0253 720911)

Patent Office, 25 Southampton Buildings, London WC1A 1AY (01-405 8721)

Office of Fair Trading, Field House, 15–25 Bream's Buildings, London EC4A 1PR (01-242 2858)

The Registrar, Stationer's Hall, London EC4M 7DD (01-253 9393)

Registrar of Trademarks, 23 Southampton Buildings, London WC2A 1AY

Society of Business Economists, 11 Bay Tree Walk, Watford WD1 3RX (0923 37287)

Society of Company and Commercial Accountants, 40 Tyndalls Park Road, Bristol BS8 1PL (0272 738261)

Venture Capital Report Ltd, Boston Road, Henley-on-Thames (0491 579999)

Local help: some examples

Community of St Helens Trust Ltd

Comprehensive advice and assistance, including premises and finance, for ventures in the district. Help with opportunities and training, loans where essential. P O Box 36, St Helens, Merseyside (0744 28882 exts 2570, 2568, 2652)

ICI Mond Division

Advice on setting up a small firm, on financial and technical problems. Help with premises. With other major employers in area, also new company (Business Links Ltd) to expand these activities. ICI Chemicals and Polymers Ltd, Merseyside Operations, Castner-Kellner Site, PO Box 9, Runcorn, Cheshire WA7 4JE (0928 514444 ext 2062)

Enterprise Lancaster

Advice and help for smaller firms in area. Information on industrial sites and buildings; low rental start-up accommodation. Small Firms Club. Information from Town Hall, Lancaster LA1 1PH (0524 65272 ext 232) contact Mr P Sandford

Enterprise North

A free, voluntary organisation offering advice and guidance to people wishing to establish new small businesses in the North of England, with eight area panels covering the North East and Cumbria. Contact: Coordinator & Liaison Officer, Durham University Business School, Mill Hill Lane, Durham DH1 3LB (091-374 2000)

Leicestershire Small Firms Centre

Helps small firms with advice and counselling, management consultancy and project terms. Seminars and courses. Help with property and planning. 30 New Walk, Leicester LE1 5DD (0533 554464)

Mendip & Wansdyke Local Enterprise Group

Information and advice on any aspect of setting up a business. Help with premises and planning. Wansdyke Enterprise Agency, High Street, Paulton, Bristol BS18 5NW (0761 415400) covers South Wansdyke. North Wansdyke comes under Pixash Lane, Keynsham, Bristol BS18 1TP (0272 867485)

Small Business Development Unit, Teesside
Advice and support for local small businesses. Research and training via Research Unit, c/o Teesside Polytechnic, Borough Road, Middlesbrough, Cleveland (0642 218121)

Premises

In addition to the 'advance factory' programme already in operation, the English Industrial Estates Corporation, in conjunction with the Department of Trade and Industry, is building small workshop premises in areas of high unemployment. Enquiries can be made direct to the EIEC, Team Valley, Gateshead, Tyne and Wear NE11 0NA (091-487 8941) or to the Department of Trade and Industry's regional offices.

Labour relations & personnel management

Advisory Conciliation & Arbitration Service (ACAS)
Provide a free, comprehensive advisory service on request to employers through their officers based in Scotland, Wales and nine regional offices in England. Head Office: 27 Wilton Street, London SW1X 7AZ (01-210 3000)

Local small business clubs

These aim to further interest in small businesses by the exchange of ideas, promotion, advice and support.

National associations representing small firms

Association of British Chambers of Commerce
Co-ordination of views of industry and commerce on matters of national and international importance and presents them to government. Sovereign House, 212a Shaftesbury Avenue, London WC2H 8EW (01-240 5831)

Association of Independent Businesses
Concerned with protecting the interests of businesses including unquoted public companies. Trowbray House, 108 Western Street, London SE1 3QB (01-403 4066)

Confederation of British Industry (CBI)
Represents and co-ordinates the views of small firms in its membership. Financial, economic and fiscal matters, industrial training, labour relations, technical legislation, company and commercial law. Centre Point, 103 New Oxford Street, London WC1A 1DD (01-379 7400)

Smaller Firms Council
Centre Point, 103 New Oxford Street, London WC1A 1DD (01-379 7400)

Federation of Medium and Small Enterprises
Industrial planning advice, representation before Industrial Disputes Tribunal. Planning help in setting up consultative machinery.
Enterprise House, Henley-on-Thames, Oxon RG9 1TU (0491 576161)

The Forum of Private Business Ltd
Represents and co-ordinates the views of small and medium sized privately owned enterprises, including proprietors.
Ruskin Chambers, Drury Lane, Knutsford WA16 0ED (0565 4468)

National Chamber of Trade
Represents and co-ordinates the views of retailing, distributive trades and service industries in membership of the constituent chambers of trade and commerce.
Enterprise House, Henley-on-Thames, Oxon RG9 1TU (0491 576161)

National Federation of Self-Employed and Small Businesses Ltd
Represents and co-ordinates the views of self-employed persons. 32 St Anne's Road West, Lytham St Annes, Lancs (0253 720911)

The Small Business Bureau
32 Smith Square, London SW1P 3HH (01-222 0330)

Some specialist libraries

British Institute of Management Library
Management House, Cottingham Road, Corby, Northants NN17 1TT (0536 204222)

Department of Industry Library
Ashdown House, 123 Victoria Street, London SW1E 6RB
Prior appointment only. Covers industrial technology, industrial development, management of research and development, science policy.

Institute of Marketing Library
Moor Hall, Cookham, Berkshire SL6 9QH (06285 24922)

Department of Trade Library
1–19 Victoria Street, London SW1H 0ET (01-215 4250)
Prior appointment only. Covers descriptive economics, including commercial organisations throughout the world.

London Business School Library
Sussex Place, Regent's Park, London NW1 4SA (01-262 5050)
Books and periodicals on all aspects of management, also business, economics, sociology, business law and related topics. Information files. Annual reports, press comments and some stockbrokers' reports on British and overseas companies.

City University Business School Library
Frobisher Crescent, London EC2Y 8HB (01-920 0111)
Similar to LBS collection.

City of London Polytechnic Library
School of Business Studies, 84 Moorgate, London EC2M 6SQ (01-283 1030)
Similar to LBS collection.

Monopolies and Mergers Commission Library
New Court, 48 Carey Street, London WC2A 2JT (01-324 1467)
Prior appointment only. Covers monopolies and competition, salary surveys and industrial economics.

Office of Fair Trading Library
Field House, Bream's Buildings, London EC4A 1PR (01-242 2858)
Prior appointment only. Covers consumer affairs, consumer credit, monopolies, mergers and restrictive practices.

Science Reference Library
25 Southampton Buildings, Chancery Lane, London WC2A 1AW (01-636 1544)
Contains those British reports on industrial markets received by copyright deposit which are publicly available (about 10 per cent of the total). Statistics covering particular industries or products. Trade directories and journals.

Statistics and Market Intelligence Library
1 Victoria Street, London SW1 (01-215 7877)
Comprehensive collection of UK and overseas statistics, some commercially published market surveys.

Business Statistics Office
Cardiff Road, Newport, Gwent NP1 1XG (0633 815696)
An office of the Department of Trade and Industry. Library contains material on statistical methodology and UK official statistics – much material also available in London. The statistical staff can occasionally assist in expanding the figures given in the various *Business Monitor* series.

Index of Advertisers

Index

Note. References in italics indicate figures or tables